Praise for *Fiddle:*
One Woman, Four Strings, and 8,000 Miles of Music

"Vivian Wagner's debut memoir takes us on a journey across the country of fiddling and into its heart. Along the way, the young woman, who was trained in classical violin—how to play by the rules—embarks on 'an affair with fiddling' that teaches her a new music, a music of grit, improvisation, and raw energy."

—**Rebecca McClanahan**, author of
The Riddle Song and Other Rememberings

"*Fiddle* is a uniquely compelling journey that left me wishing I was a better writer. Vivian Wagner is that writer. Charming, smart, lyrical and surprising, I recommend it to anyone— savage beast or not—who needs their soul soothed."

—**Suzanne Finnamore**, international
bestselling author of *Split*

"Irish, Scottish, bluegrass, old-time, klezmer, western swing, Cajun: such are the stops along Vivian Wagner's quest to learn about fiddle playing at a time when her life is changing. Elegantly wrought, *Fiddle* plucks the heartstrings with its story of improvisation, adaptation, and the resilience of the human spirit."

—**Lee Martin**, author of *From Our House* and *River of Heaven*

"*Fiddle* is more than a musical coming of age. It's a story of personal salvation as American as its Appalachian setting, and the notes it hits are deep and pure and hopeful."

—**David Goodwillie**, author of *American Subversive*

fiddle

*One Woman, Four Strings,
and 8,000 Miles of Music*

Vivian Wagner

CITADEL PRESS
Kensington Publishing Corp.
www.kensingtonbooks.com

CITADEL PRESS BOOKS are published by

Kensington Publishing Corp.
119 West 40th Street
New York, NY 10018

All Kensington titles, imprints, and distributed lines are available at special quantity discounts for bulk purchases for sales promotions, premiums, fund-raising, educational, or institutional use. Special book excerpts or customized printings can also be created to fit specific needs. For details, write or phone the office of the Kensington special sales manager: Kensington Publishing Corp., 119 West 40th Street, New York, NY 10018, attn: Special Sales Department; phone 1-800-221-2647.

CITADEL PRESS and the Citadel logo are Reg. U.S. Pat. & TM Off.

First printing: May 2010

10 9 8 7 6 5 4 3 2 1

Printed in the United States of America

Library of Congress Control Number: 2009937077

ISBN-13: 978-0-8065-3122-9
ISBN-10: 0-8065-3122-3

For William and Rose

You must use the body—its curves,
its hollows, the spring of the sound, which
brings back what is absent, what has
been and is now gone, fading.
                    —Sheila Black, "Violin"

The earth keeps some vibration going
There in your heart, and that is you.
And if the people find you can fiddle,
Why, fiddle you must, for all your life.
                    —Edgar Lee Masters, "Fiddler Jones"

Contents

fiddle

Chapter 1

Learning to Play

My mom always wanted me to play fiddle. She'd grown up poor, the daughter of a long line of pioneers with Scots-Irish and German roots who finally settled in California's Central Valley in the 1940s. As she packed tomatoes into crates and milked goats, she listened to transistor radios playing country and bluegrass music, which often as not featured fiddling. After high school she left farm country for Los Angeles, worked her way through college, and earned degrees in math and statistics. On her climb upward, however, she took with her some of the culture ingrained since childhood. Growing tomatoes. Putting up jam. Humming tunes. And liking fiddle music.

"You're always playing Bach and Beethoven," she'd say to me when I was in high school. "Why don't you play some fiddle tunes?"

She pronounced the "ch" and the "th" as if she'd never studied advanced German at UCLA. But somehow, pronouncing the names of German composers wrong was almost a matter of principle for her.

She did this with other words, too. Like "wash." One time a friend made fun of how I said *warsh* instead of *wash*, and immediately I realized where this came from: my mom.

So that evening over dinner, when Mom said something about *warshing* the clothes, I corrected her.

"It's *wash*, Mom," I said with all the superiority I could muster as a nine-year-old.

Her response surprised me. Instead of thanking me for my brilliance and changing her ways immediately, she looked at me, long and hard, her pale blue eyes like thin ice.

Finally, she said, "That's how I say it, and that's how it's supposed to be: *warsh*."

And that was the end of it.

The fact is, though, I didn't know anything about fiddling. I'd never heard it, and if Mom liked it, well, then, it must have been something pretty okie. That's what my dad often called my mom, teasingly. *Okie.* I never knew quite what it meant, but it sounded pretty bad. Whatever it was, I didn't want to be it.

And anyway, I was a *violinist.*

Some part of me wanted to please my mom, though, to play something that she might like. So one day at the music store with my dad, I saw some fiddle books: *Bluegrass Fiddle Styles,* by Stacy Phillips and Kenny Kosek, and *The Fiddle Book* by Marion Thede. I asked him if he could buy them for me, thinking it might make my mom happy if I tried to play from them. Reluctantly, he agreed. He used his own allowance money, which came from his travel reimbursement checks at work, and paid $15 in cash for the two books.

When we got home, I showed my mom the books.

"So let's hear some," she said. "Go ahead and play."

"I'll need to practice first," I said, shy and unsure of myself or fiddle music. I tried to make sense of the strange cross-tunings and notations in these books. I tried to understand how to play "Cotton-Eyed Joe," "Old Dan Tucker," and "Tom and Jerry." But I didn't have any recordings of fiddle music, didn't know what it sounded like, and couldn't make much sense of this music. It all seemed so foreign to me, and I couldn't compare it to the watered-down classical music I'd been learning in lessons and in the school orchestra. So the books stayed on the shelf in my bedroom, unused and forgotten, and I never did play any of those tunes for my mom.

∽

My love of violin had started when I was seven and first heard Elaine Moreno playing. After school at the Navy ranch house of my babysitter, Mrs. Moreno, I'd sit on the couch and listen to her teenage daughter practice. Elaine would swing her thick, glossy black hair through the air, twirling across the living room floor, smiling, at one with the music.

Whatever magic she possessed, I wanted.

So in fourth grade, when my teacher sent home a little pink mimeographed slip with information about the school orchestra, I begged my mom to let me play violin. She agreed, and I joined, dutifully carrying my rental violin back and forth to school, adding my interpretation of "Hot Cross Buns" and "Jingle Bells" to the cacophony of beginning violins, violas, and cellos.

During the summers after fourth and fifth grade, my mom signed me up for lessons with Miss Blakesley, who lived in the California desert town of Ridgecrest, where I went to school, in a trailer cluttered with music books, magazines, houseplants, and cat toys. In her living room window, an air conditioner kept up a continual, comforting whir. She taught the Suzuki violin method, starting with that anthem of beginning violinists everywhere, "Twinkle, Twinkle Little Star," and its variations: taka-taka-ta-ka, and taka-taka-taka-taka. Eventually we moved on to "Lightly Row" and "The Happy Farmer." Shinichi Suzuki developed the Suzuki method in Japan as a way to teach children music through immersion, saturation, and ear training, and it emphasized recitals and group playing. Miss Blakesley arranged regular, Suzuki-style recitals for her beginning students to play their pieces together in neat rows, but she also used the Suzuki music books to teach her students how to read music. And in her weekly lessons, we worked slowly but surely through *Suzuki Book I*.

I learned one main thing in these early lessons: violin is hard. To begin with, there's the way you hold the instrument and the way you hold the bow. Hold either one wrong, and your teacher will tell you, in no uncertain terms, that you will never be able to play beautiful music. So, wanting to play beautiful music, you focus on bending your thumb on the bow just so, placing your pinky just so, holding your left wrist just so, and bending your fingers onto the fingerboard just so. As soon as you focus on one, though, another inevitably goes out of whack. Bend your right thumb, and your left wrist creeps up. Hold your left wrist down, and your left fingers flatten on the strings, your right thumb straightens, and your right pinky flies off into space.

All this happens before there's any consideration of *sound*, let alone *music*. That comes lessons and lessons later, when you work on tone, and pitch, and the pressure of the bow on the strings, and the running of the bow hairs parallel to the bridge, and all the other thousand things that you must learn to do if you ever want to make beautiful music.

I played and played, most of the time getting it wrong, but after every lesson, getting it a little more right. Miss Blakesley gave me a sticker for each piece I completed, and I especially liked the strawberry scratch-and-sniff ones. My sister, Ann, who took lessons with me, favored plum. She liked it so much that she peeled one off her practice sheet and stuck it on the chin rest of her tiny one-tenth-size violin, where it remains to this day, announcing its cheerful message of "Great job!," the paper worn thin but still smelling faintly fruity. Ann's lesson came before mine. While she played, I waited, sitting on the brown plaid couch, reading a book, looking at an old issue of *Reader's Digest*, or just gazing out the window at the trailer next door. Ann often got frustrated, and Miss Blakesley would end the lesson early, looking over at me exasperatedly. But I sympathized with my sister. Though five years older, and a bit more patient, I knew.

Violin was hard.

Really hard.

Eventually, Ann gave up violin for cello. I kept with it, though, taking lessons, going to orchestra practice, and gradually improving. In junior high and high school, my friends and I listened to Journey, The Cars, The Who, and Pink Floyd, but secretly, I really loved the music we played in orchestra. I loved Bach, Corelli, Barber, Stravinsky. In high school, I worked my way up from fourth chair, to third, to second, and finally, in my senior year, to concert mistress. I loved how the music flowed through me and around me, and I relished orchestra's peculiar combination of competition and art. Orchestra was my home, my second family. My best friend, Michele, played cello, and we hung around each other all the time, before, during, and after orchestra practice, our friendship growing out of our shared love of orchestra.

I grew up on land my parents had bought in the early 1970s in the Sierra Nevada Mountains, about thirty miles from Ridgecrest, where I went to school. On weekends at home, I liked to take my violin down by the creek, prop a green and off-white book of Bach's unaccompanied violin sonatas up on a rough granite boulder, and play. My music echoed through the canyon, into the wilderness beyond. The sun heated the wood of my violin, and I smelled the rosin on my bow, which was the same smell as the pitch from the piñon trees that covered the mountains by our house, pitch that covered my hands with dark splotches when Ann and I searched for piñon nuts, digging them out of the small, stiff cones. The violin's wood smelled like the pine, maple, and willow trees all around me. And the horsehair bow, warmed in the sun, smelled like the tail of Trixie, our horse, when she stood in the sun in the meadow, swishing at flies. Playing my violin there by the creek brought all these elements of my life together, and at the same time it took me beyond them, into a realm of pure music, pure light, pure beauty.

It was such difficult music, though. Bach's unaccompanied sonatas have triple and quadruple stops, three or four notes played at a time in impossibly complex chords, sixteenth- and thirty-second notes swirling like a raging, black river across the page. I loved those pieces so much that I'd try, over and over, to play them, knowing exactly what I wanted the music to sound like. I knew my interpretation was only approximate, but I kept trying.

Sometimes, when Bach got *too* hard, my eyes wandered from the page, and I'd play new notes and melodies, improvising on his basic melodies and chords. My notes, now my truly *mine*, wandered on the pine-scented air through the canyon, echoing off the granite cliffs.

∞

As a freshman at UC Irvine, I signed up for orchestra, which allowed me to receive free private lessons with a violin professor. At my first lesson, the kindly looking, white-haired professor asked me to play something for him. I brought out my book of beloved Bach sonatas, placing it tentatively on the black music stand next to his wooden shelf heavy with theory and history books. I turned to a movement in Sonata IV called "Ciaccona," one of the most beautiful, and most difficult, pieces in the whole Bach repertoire. I'd never really mastered any of these sonatas, and out in the woods, by my home, that didn't matter. But here, with a real violin professor, it did.

As I played, I put everything I had—my heart, my soul, my whole body—into the music. *I must really be impressing him,* I thought. I swayed and strained, yearning for the music I knew Bach intended. I was so deeply involved in my interpretation of Bach's bewildering beauty that it took me a moment to feel the professor's hand tapping my shoulder.

"Okay, okay," he said. "That's fine now. Okay."

He spoke in the tones one uses to comfort an accident victim. "That's a difficult piece for you, no?" he said.

I nodded meekly.

"And I see that you love it very much."

I nodded again in vigorous agreement, not quite seeing where he was going with this.

"But you shouldn't play it."

I stared at him, aghast. Didn't he hear what I had been playing? The beautiful music? Bach, for God's sake? The *"Ciaccona"*? What didn't he understand? What kind of professor *was* he, anyway?

"For you, it's too hard," he went on coldly, methodically, as if diagnosing the probable cause of death in a cadaver. "You need to work on technique. You need to work on skills. And I don't think that piece is what you need to work on now."

I went back for a few more lessons with him, and I stayed in orchestra until the end of the semester. But I felt defeated, and before long I put my violin away and didn't crack open its case for many years.

∞

I studied English in college and moved to Ohio for graduate school at Ohio State. I met a lovely twenty-one-year-old boy in Larry's Bar, near the university. He was an undergraduate student at Ohio State, and he had long, blond hair and wore a black leather jacket, looking like a cross between a biker and a choir boy. I was smitten by his sweet badness, by his intelligence, by his daringness. In one of our early conversations at Larry's I told him I played violin, and so for our first date he arranged for us to see the Columbus Symphony, which played Tchaikovsky's "Serenade for Strings" and Vivaldi's "Spring." We dated for a few months, and then, impulsively, we got married one cold January day at the downtown courthouse. We were young, and we had no clear sense of what we were doing or why. I'd left just about everything—my childhood, my family, my past—behind in California. In fact, one of the few things I *had* brought with me from childhood was my violin. My instrument had accompanied me all the way to Ohio, crammed with my books and Apple computer into my Mustang, and it would continue to accompany me into the future. I didn't often play it, but I kept it with me, a constant companion.

I saw marriage, even to a relative stranger, as a way to bring stability to my life. A way to set up a new home in this distant land. A way to grow up. Though we barely knew each other when we married, over time we became close friends and partners. We worked our way through graduate school, eventually moving to Illinois to get our PhDs. Just as we were finishing our degrees, he got a job at Muskingum College in New Concord, Ohio. Neither of us had ever heard of the college, which has since changed its name to Muskingum University, or of New Concord, but we were game for anything. He accepted the job, and we made plans to move and start a new phase of our life.

Before we moved there, I studied the map of southeastern Ohio, looking at the crooked roads indicating hills, the names of villages and towns dotting the landscape: Norwich, Zanesville, Cambridge, Roseville, Crooksville, Barnesville. Southeastern Ohio is just on the edges of Appalachia, in the hilly, unglaciated part of the state. I read about the area's history, how it had been strip-mined throughout the nineteenth and early twentieth centuries, how it was the poorest part of the state, how it was classified as Appalachia by the federal government.

Driving our U-Haul truck from Illinois, I was struck once we got past Columbus by the beauty of the green, rolling hills that seemed to go on forever; the picturesque farm houses and grazing cattle; the winding rural roads; the village with its main street, gas station, grocery store, hardware store, and post office. We bought a little white and blue-shuttered house on the western edge of the village, on a narrow street that climbed steeply up from Route 40, or the Old National Road, which cuts through the village.

In the first couple of years of living in New Concord, we had two children, William and Rose, and I stayed home with them, doing freelance writing in my basement office while my husband taught at the college. The village seemed like a perfect place to raise a family, a perfect place to call our home.

It didn't take me long to realize, though, that I was an outsider in southeastern Ohio. Down at Shegog's IGA, the grocery store on Main Street, everyone seemed to know everyone else by name. People in the village spoke with rough, Appalachian accents, and they viewed newcomers with wariness and suspicion. The few people I got to know in those early years were affiliated with the college, but at that time most of the college faculty were middle-aged or older, so I felt just about as isolated from them as I did from the longtime residents of the village. I felt like I didn't really know this place. And I began to realize that no matter how long I lived there, I'd never be from 'round here.

I stayed home with the kids, keeping to myself, tending to their needs. I tried to make a home in a place that felt like a wilderness outpost. I shopped at Shegog's; I went to the post office; I bought supplies at the hardware store, pushing first one child and then the other around the village in a dark blue Graco stroller. I tried my best to make a happy, stable home for our family. The kind of home I'd always wanted. The home I'd been wanting ever since we married in the courthouse on that January day so many years before.

Once the kids got a little older, I began teaching journalism at the college, happy to finally have a full-time job, a growing career. But I always had a nagging suspicion that somehow, I didn't belong to the landscape, to the culture. That I wasn't a native. Something about the home, and the life we were building, always felt temporary. There's a wall between those who live in Appalachia and those who move there, and I began to think that perhaps that wall would never be breached.

Occasionally, over the years, I pulled out my violin, rosined up my bow, and played in concerts with the Southeastern Ohio Symphony Orchestra or *Messiah* performances at a church in

Zanesville. But most of the time my trusty old violin stayed in my closet, leaning up against the wall, waiting for those times, few and far between, when I opened its case, rosined up the bow, and took it for a spin.

For the last years of her life, my mom was sick with emphysema, bed bound, hooked up to oxygen, and close to death. One summer night, about nine years after we moved to New Concord, she slipped into a coma and died.

Reeling with grief, confused, and alone, I flew back to the California desert to bury my mom. While arranging the funeral, Ann and I came up with the idea of playing some kind of music for the service. Though we could barely hold ourselves together enough to organize the funeral and write up an obituary, let alone perform, we told ourselves it would be a fitting tribute to her, since she had insisted on all those music lessons, come to all of our school concerts, and encouraged us in our music.

Perhaps we suspected, though, that playing through the funeral would help us cope. Playing, we could focus on notes, and not thoughts. Playing, we'd have rhythm and pitch and phrasing as a grammar for our grief. Grief was startlingly, frighteningly new, but music was a language we'd spent our lifetimes learning.

We had both left our instruments at home, though. We hadn't even considered bringing them. So, the day before the funeral we sat in the Starbucks on China Lake Boulevard, drinking caramel frappuccinos, watching the traffic, looking at the tumbleweeds piled in the desert lot by the pizza place across the street, considering our options. We talked of calling an old music teacher. We debated looking up friends who had played in orchestra with us. Finally, though, we called a music store and asked about rentals.

I explained to the man who answered the phone that we wanted to rent a cello and a violin for a few days so we could practice and then perform at our mom's funeral.

"We don't do short-term rentals," he said.

"Oh," I said, my voice trailing off. "Okay."

I heard him pause and breathe on the other end of the line.

"*Usually*," he said. "We *usually* don't do short-term rentals. But I'll let you do it for this."

"Thank you so much," I said. "You don't know how much this means to us."

"That's fine," he said. "Just come down to the store."

So we did, and he pulled out new, shiny instruments for us, set up music stands, and told us we could play as long as we wanted, right there in the middle of the store. Ann and I looked at each other, unable to believe his generosity, offering us both rental instruments and a practice space.

We sat in the middle of the music store and played. We played Bach and Mozart, hymns and popular songs. We played that old high school orchestra standby that we knew so well, Pachelbel's Canon. We pulled out a wedding songbook from the music store's shelf, since we couldn't find a funeral songbook, and we played love songs from its contents. Ann and I played until our fingers hurt, until we couldn't play anymore. Finally, exhausted and spent, we decided we'd play the Pachelbel, and one of the wedding songs. And at the end, Ann would play "Danny Boy," because Mom used to like it when she played that song.

On the morning of the funeral, out in the desert cemetery under a tent, we set up our instruments near the end of Mom's pine coffin, which had purple, blue, and white wildflowers strewn on top. Surrounded by the hot, bright desert, in front of Dad and a few of my parents' friends, we played. Just like we'd practiced:

Pachelbel, love song, "Danny Boy." Somehow, we got through it. Somehow, we stayed with the program. We played, and then we spoke at the little wooden podium, and then we sat back down and played some more. And as we played, our notes resonated through the dry desert heat, across the sand, and out toward the distant volcanic hills.

∞

I lined up violin lessons for the kids when William was seven and Rose was five, with a young woman named Angela. She gave lessons on Thursday afternoons in the basement of St. Benedict's Catholic Church in Cambridge, a town just east of New Concord. I rented a violin for William, and Rose played the same tenth-size violin Ann had played many years before. After a few months, Rose insisted that violin was just too hard, and she decided to quit. William, though, stuck with it.

His lessons with Angela continued for a couple of years, once a week, every week, William marching through the Suzuki books just like I had. His lessons were much like my own had been: long, difficult, and repetitive. It takes a long time to make anything like music on the violin. He worked hard at it, though, his blond head bobbing up and down while he stretched his fingers to play the notes. Some days he'd get frustrated, and many days in between lessons he didn't want to practice. He seemed to want to continue the lessons, though, so I kept taking him. During his lessons, Rose and I sat on little folding chairs off to the side. She'd color pictures, and I'd read a book or absentmindedly stare at the scuffed, cracked linoleum.

One day, though, the year after my mom died, and the summer I turned forty, something happened that brought me to attention.

"Want to learn some fiddle?" I heard her ask William, a hint of Appalachian lilt in her voice. She tossed her straight brown hair back, looking at him brightly, defiantly.

"Sure," he said. "I guess so."

She pulled out *Mel Bay's Deluxe Fiddling Method,* by Craig Duncan, a spiral-bound music book with a happy-looking man in a plaid flannel shirt fiddling on the cover.

"I have this book, and we could play a little from it," she said. "I grew up playing fiddle with my grandpa, and I think you might like it."

She turned to the first song in the book, "Bile Them Cabbage Down."

"Let's start with this one," she said. "I'll play it through first, and then you can try."

She played through the little tune, with its double-stops and simple bowing pattern. And while she played, I watched and, for the first time in one of his lessons, *listened.*

"See?" she showed William. "It's just second finger on the A string, and then third finger." She played through the first few measures, and William copied her. Then a few more, and he copied again.

At the end of the lesson, while William put his violin away, I went over to give Angela her $12 check.

"I might want to learn some of that fiddling," I said nonchalantly, noncommittally, not wanting to reveal how much, suddenly and inexplicably, *I* wanted to learn to play fiddle. I *really* wanted to learn fiddle. I wanted to fiddle more, perhaps, than William did. Fiddling suddenly seemed vitally important, even necessary, for me to learn. Perhaps it had to do with grief for my mom's death, and with the fact that I was just starting to feel the inklings of a midlife crisis coming on. All I knew consciously, though, was that I *had* to learn it.

"Okay," she said, looking at me a little strangely. "You can play along, if you want."

And so at the next lesson, I brought along my violin. William, Angela, and I played a bit together after the Suzuki part of each lesson. I could tell William thought it kind of odd that Mom was joining in, but he seemed to take it in stride. Over a few weeks, we worked more on "Bile Them Cabbage Down," and then progressed to "Ida Red," "Old Joe Clark," and my favorite, "Devil's Dream," a whirlwind of sixteenth notes that sounded really quite fiddle-y. At home, he and I practiced our new tunes together, and the fact that I played along seemed not to bother him. It actually seemed to make practicing more fun for him. If Mom liked playing violin, well, then, maybe he did, too.

And as I played through those fiddle tunes, something strange began to happen. My fingers running through the melodies and the double-stops, my bow scratching out centuries of folk music transcribed and simplified for beginners, I felt like I'd found something I hadn't even known I'd lost.

Chapter 2

Mountain Heir

On a hot Saturday afternoon, my husband, kids, and I headed east out of New Concord on Interstate 70 in our Honda Odyssey, before exiting south and going deep into Ohio's hill country, first on a narrow paved road, next a gravel road, and then a dirt road. We passed stretches of thick woods, trailers, pickup trucks, and dogs tied to trees with lengths of rusty chain.

"Where are we going again?" Rose asked, always curious about what we were up to, and why.

"It's a bluegrass festival," I said, not really knowing how to explain bluegrass to her. I wasn't sure *I* even knew what it was. A few weeks earlier I'd told my dentist, who played mandolin in a band, that I'd been learning to play fiddle. He mentioned the Mountain Heir Bluegrass Festival, down in the countryside outside of Old Washington. After a couple of Google missteps, as I looked for "Mountain Air" and "Mountain Hair," I finally found it: Mountain *Heir*, held at the Old National Trail Campground. It intrigued me. I'd never been to a bluegrass festival, but I thought it might be a chance to catch some fiddling, and to explore the Appalachian hills that were still pretty mysterious to me, even after all these years of living in southeastern Ohio.

I turned forty that summer, and though I didn't fully realize it at the time, I was on the edge of a midlife crisis. I was evaluating myself, and my life, thinking about what direction I wanted to head in the future. I was happy enough with my life, with being a wife, a mom, and a professor, but I had a feeling that there was more I could do. More I could explore. More I could learn. And though I didn't quite know why, fiddling seemed to hold the key to this self-exploration.

This festival, I'd thought, would be a chance to investigate fiddling, and also to expose the kids to fiddling. I thought it might be good for them to be exposed to the music, culture, and people right around them in Appalachia. So, I'd convinced them and my husband to go along with me to check out the festival. Somewhat reluctantly, they agreed, and there we were, bumping along on a dirt road headed into the wilderness.

"A *bluegrass* festival?" William asked. "Is there going to be any music we like there?"

"I don't know, William," I said, feeling exasperated. He liked Coldplay, Muse, the Beatles. Sure, he played violin, and we'd been playing the fiddle music with Angela, but that wasn't the kind of music he wanted to listen to on a summer afternoon. I looked back at him, slumping in his seat with exaggerated boredom. I could almost hear his thought: *Mom's lost it.* Even Rose, in her sweet way, looked at me curiously.

"We're going to see what we see, and that's it," I said firmly, matter-of-factly, as if *I* had any idea what we would see. Besides, it wouldn't do any of us any harm to try something new.

Rose shrugged. "Okay," she said, happy to be along for the ride.

William sighed melodramatically, turned up the volume on his iPod, and looked out the window at the run-down wooden shacks, cars on blocks, and outside dogs. Usually when we went anywhere, we went to Cleveland to see their grandparents, or the Colony Square Mall in Zanesville to see a movie, or to Ruby Tuesday in Cambridge. *Not* to backwoods campgrounds.

"Are you *sure* you know where we're going?" my husband asked, glancing at the MapQuest printout I held on my lap.

"Yeah," I said, though I wasn't sure at all. "It's up here; just keep following this road."

He kept driving on a road that had become just two tire tracks through the dry grass. Finally, we arrived at the Old National Trail Campground.

As we drove in, we saw rows of RVs, and the air through the open windows of our van smelled thick with the wood-smoke from campfires. We parked and got out, following the sound of bluegrass music up and over the hill to a shady area where mostly seniors sat on lawn chairs. They were listening to a band playing on a makeshift trailer stage. I immediately realized our mistake: we hadn't brought any chairs. I asked one of the women working at the concession stand if she knew where we could find some.

"Just a minute, I have a few in our trailer," she said, eyeing me as the outsider I felt I was, but with a look suggesting I wouldn't be one for long if I just proved myself in some way I didn't quite understand. "How many do you need?"

Embarrassed that I hadn't thought of bringing chairs, I sheepishly told her four. She smiled, looking at me and then at my less-than-enthusiastic family, and said she'd be right back.

Borrowed camp chairs in hand, we settled down to listen to the music. We were surrounded by toe-tapping, John Deere cap–wearing men and tough-looking women in jeans and T-shirts, all of them with lawn and camp chairs that they'd had sense enough to bring themselves, sipping coffee, eating pie, and listening intently to the fiddle playing and banjo plucking. There under the pine trees and maple trees of the Ohio woods, just a few miles from New Concord, we had entered a different world, a mysterious realm, a place rooted in these hills for as long as anyone here could remember.

The first act we saw, Melvin Goins and his band, had a fiddler. As the band played its lineup of country and bluegrass songs, I was entranced by the way the fiddler's fingers ran up and down the fingerboard, the way the music came out of him as naturally as wind blowing through the pines. The more interested I became, though, the more impatient William grew, leaning back in his chair, sighing, tapping his sister on the shoulder.

"When are we going to *go*?" William whispered loudly to me.

"After a while," I said. "Just enjoy the music."

He rolled his eyes and kicked the dirt. Rose giggled, looking over at me and quieting down when I gave her a look that said *shush*. My husband sat there stoically in his lawn chair, glancing over at me and the kids when we started whispering.

"Want to walk with them around the campground for a bit?" I begged him. "Please?"

He looked at me just as William had a moment earlier, and I was struck, not for the first time, by the similarities between my husband and our son. Both were charismatic and boyish, with blond hair and a natural attractiveness, as well as a tendency toward frustration when things weren't exactly right, exactly perfect. And it occurred to me, looking at my family, that maybe it had been a bad idea to bring them all along to this festival. Maybe I should have just come myself. It had been my crazy idea, anyway.

"I guess," he said. "Come on, kids."

He walked off with them to the edge of the audience area, and the kids scurried around under the pine trees, picking up sticks, looking at holes in the trees. He stood nearby, his arms crossed, glancing over at me now and then. Sitting there alone, I turned back to the music and listened, entranced, to the notes cascading out of that fiddle. I was amazed by the way the fiddle player picked up melodies and riffed on them as if such improvisation were the easiest, most natural thing in the world.

And in that moment, I fell in love with fiddling.

After the band wrapped up its set, I walked over to where the fiddle player had gone to the side of the stage. John Rigsby, he said his name was when I introduced myself. He seemed surprised by my interest, and shy, looking at his feet now and then, scratching the campground dirt. He told me that he lived down near Martha, Kentucky, that he also played mandolin and sang, and that he had played off and on with the Melvin Goins band for a few years. In his blue-and-red-plaid shirt and jeans, he had dark-cropped hair and the demeanor of someone comfortable in his skin, comfortable with his profession, happy with his performance, and slightly flattered by my questions—though he didn't seem to much fathom what I hoped to find out by talking with him. Honestly, I didn't know myself.

He told me he'd played fiddle since he was nine. I told him that I played violin, and he looked at me curiously, the beginnings of a smile wavering on his lips.

"Is that right?" he said, his words rolling out in a slight Kentucky drawl.

"Just violin," I said. "But I'm trying to learn fiddle."

"You know how to read music?" he asked, eyeing me rather like the concession woman had a while earlier.

Surprised, and not sure if this was a trick question, I said, "Yeah, don't you?"

He looked at me, bemused, smiling broadly now, as if he were letting me in on a fairly open secret.

"Nope," he said. "Do it all by ear."

I stared at him, stunned. All by ear? All that music? How could that be? How could he not know how to read music and play so well?

Almost conciliatory, he said, "Want to see my fiddle?"

"Sure," I said. "I'd love to."

I followed him back to the band's trailer, this time with Rose, who'd left William and my husband to run over to join us, interested to see what Mommy was up to. John carefully took out the black leather fiddle case and opened it up on a stump by the truck. Then he pulled out one of the strangest fiddles I'd ever seen: a five-string fiddle with a ram's head carved in great detail in place of a scroll, the horns curving down on the side, the eyes staring hard out at anyone who might pick up the instrument, as if saying, *So let's see what kind of fiddle you play. Let's just see.* I stared at the ram's head, considering the challenge inherent in the glint of its ebony eyes, the deep shine of its wood.

"Wow," I said. "That's a beautiful instrument."

Rose looked at it, pointing to the scroll.

"Look at the eyes," she said. "*Weird.*"

"It's got a nice, deep sound," he said. "Not too loud a fiddle."

He himself was also soft-spoken, but he clearly loved this fiddle, and loved talking about things related to fiddle.

"Any more, that's all I play," he said.

He handed me the instrument, and I took it gingerly, not sure what to do.

"Go ahead; try it," he said.

I bowed a few notes, mostly open strings, unable to think of any of the fiddle tunes I'd been learning from the *Mel Bay* book, and suddenly shy, worried about measuring up. Plus, there was that ram's head. I felt it looking at me, up from the scroll. I played a few scales starting on the low C fifth-string, which made the instrument something of a cross between a violin and the lower-keyed viola.

"It's lovely," I stammered, because it was. Rich and full, just like he'd said.

"Yeah, it's a remarkable instrument," he said.

I looked inside the f-hole for the label that would tell me who made it.

"It's an Arthur Conner fiddle," he said before I could locate the little label in the bright sunlight. "Down in Virginia."

I nodded, reading the label: Arthur Conner, Copper Hill, Virginia.

"So he makes fiddles down there?" I asked.

"Yup," he said. "He's gettin' pretty old, but he's still making them, near as I can tell."

I thought about Copper Hill, Virginia, envisioning hillsides covered in copper-flaked rocks and thick woods. It seemed like a magical, mystical place. And as I stood there, looking at that fiddle, I began to formulate a plan.

John and I shook hands, and I thanked him for his time.

"Sure thing," he said, placing the fiddle away carefully in its case like he was putting a baby to sleep in its crib.

Chapter 3

The Fiddle Maker

Once home, I couldn't put the thought of that fiddle out of my head. I dreamed of those ram's eyes, daring me to do *something*, though I didn't know what. That fiddle struck a chord deep within me. It was a challenge, a promise, and a mystery, all wrapped into one. I wondered about Copper Hill, Virginia. I wanted, more than anything, to find the man who had made that fiddle. I Googled Arthur Conner and tracked down his phone number. Then, partly just to have an excuse to call him and arrange a visit, I queried the magazine *Bluegrass Unlimited* about doing a profile story about Conner and his fiddles. The magazine's editor agreed to look at the story on spec, and that was enough for me, since it gave me a reason to give Conner a call and arrange a meeting. But I knew the story was just an excuse: I really wanted to meet the man who had made that beautiful fiddle. I wanted to discover its secret. To discover, perhaps, the secret of fiddling itself. It seemed, suddenly, vitally important that I pay a visit to the place where that ram's head fiddle had been born.

When I called his number, a sweetly Southern woman's voice answered the phone. I asked her if I could speak to Arthur Conner.

"Sure," she said. "I think he's in his workshop. Just a minute."

In his *workshop*. Just the thought of his fiddle workshop excited me.

A few moments later a grizzled man's voice came on the line. "Yes?" he said gruffly.

"Mr. Conner," I said. "I'm Vivian Wagner, and I'm working on a story about you for *Bluegrass Unlimited* magazine. I was wondering if I could set up a time to come by and visit with you for a few hours."

He was silent for a moment. *"Bluegrass Unlimited?"* he asked finally.

"Yes, sir," I said, not sure why I was resorting to "sir."

"Well then, I reckon you'll have to come on out," he said, his voice lilting. "I'll be happy to show you what I do."

I arranged for a family vacation down to Asheville, North Carolina, to visit some cousins of mine. On the way, I made plans for us to stop in Christiansburg, Virginia, for one night so I could drive into the mountains and meet with Conner. The *Bluegrass Unlimited* angle was good: at least I had a nominally work-related reason to be driving around the Blue Ridge Mountains meeting strangers.

We arrived late one afternoon at the Christiansburg Hampton Inn, in a part of town dominated by fast-food restaurants and gas stations. We checked in and took the elevator to our room.

"Who's up for going to meet a fiddle maker with me?" knowing what the response would be.

"Not me," said William.

"I'd rather go in the pool," said Rose, looking at me tentatively to see if I was going to push the point. She didn't have much of an opinion about fiddle makers, but she *loved* hotel pools.

"That's okay," I said. "You can just stay here and swim in the pool with Daddy, if you want."

"Yeah!" they both shouted in unison. Really, they *both* loved hotel pools. They could go to any hotel, anywhere, even a mile from our home, and be happy just to swim in its pool.

I looked at my husband, feeling kind of awkward and apologetic, knowing this was my thing. This was my journey, my obsession. I had arranged this trip; I had dragged them all down here; they had to just put up with it.

"Do you mind staying here with them while I drive up there?" I asked. "I'll be back in the early evening."

"I guess," he said. "Do what you have to do."

I looked at him, trying to discern his mood, his perspective. But he was inscrutable. As if he had shut part of himself down.

"Thanks," I said. "Really. Okay?"

He nodded. I got the kids into their bathing suits, and we all went down to the pool, which was surrounded by large bushes and a black cast-iron fence.

"I promise, I'll be back by early evening," I said. My husband waved slightly and then turned away from me to watch as the kids jumped in the pool. I waved at them, and they waved back, smiling wet smiles.

"See you kids soon!" I called. "Love you."

As I drove past the McDonald's, pizza places, and chain hotels, the late afternoon light spread green, gold, and copper on the hills. The road I drove up into the Blue Ridge Mountains would, according to MapQuest, change names several times: first Route 460, then South Franklin, then Pilot Road, High Rock Hill Road, Daniel's Run Road, Hummingbird Lane, and finally Conner Road.

I tried to note each name change as I passed the occasional crooked road sign, all the time climbing higher and higher, past old log cabins and farmhouses with towers of tomatoes, past trailers set into hills cut away to reveal millennia of yellow and rustcolored rock layers, past trucks with shotgun racks and stars-and-bars bumper stickers. At last, I arrived at Conner Road, a road named after the first settlers in these parts, ancestors, I presumed, of Conner himself.

As I drove up, Conner stood in the doorway of his modest ranch house backed up against the Virginia woods, waving. He was a wizened old man, his face like a precise, wrinkled carving from the same red maple he used to make his violins. He wore a blue plaid shirt, black suspenders, khaki pants, and a tan and green cap with a fiddle embroidered on it. He had a gray beard and mustache, reddish skin, and a broad, toothy grin.

"You made it," he called as I stepped out of the van.

"Yeah," I said. "I just kept driving."

"Well, that's the way you do it," he said, laughing a deep, scratchy, woodsy laugh.

I walked through the grass toward the house. Several large butterfly bushes heavy with purple blooms and covered with black, blue, and purple swallowtails lined the front of his house. When I approached, they flocked into the air, hovered for a moment, and then landed on nearby branches.

He led me into his home, and as my eyes gradually adjusted to the inside light, I saw wood everywhere: knotty wood paneling, a carved wooden owl gazing across the small room from his perch on a wooden mantel, and a large reddish string bass and a cello resting on a wood floor.

"This is Ilene, my wife," he said, nodding at the kind-looking woman who stood quietly at the edge of the room. She had short gray hair, a kindly face, and sharp, sprightly blue eyes.

"Nice to meet you," I said, shaking her hand.

She smiled. "The same," she said. I'd find out later that she'd known Conner her entire life, growing up just down the road from him, but they'd only married recently after both of their first spouses had died.

I felt both of them looking at me, sizing me up, a feeling I'd get used to on this journey.

"Care for something to drink?" Ilene said.

"No, that's fine," I said, getting ready to ask Conner some questions about his fiddle making, waiting for him to sit down. But he didn't. He stood there, watching me.

"Mind if I ask you a few questions before we begin?" he asked.

I was surprised. I'd worked as a journalist for years, but I wasn't used to being on the other side of an interview.

"Sure," I said.

"Well, to be honest, I could spend days talking to you about fiddles," he said. "Guess I'm just wonderin' what you want to know. What you already know."

I paused. "Well," I said. "I play violin. So I know a little already. But I'm still learning about fiddles and fiddling. I guess I want to find out everything I can about fiddles and fiddle making in a few hours."

He studied me carefully. "Play the violin, do you?" he asked.

I nodded.

"Well, maybe later I'll give you a little fiddle lesson," he said.

"That would be great," I said.

He still didn't sit down, but he pointed at a large leather-bound book on the coffee table in front of me, with *The Secrets of Stradivari* printed on the front in gold.

"That's how it all began," he said. "Most of what I know, I learned from that book."

He opened it and showed me diagrams of violins, with measurements for width, length, thickness of wood, and page after page of fine-print instructions.

"See?" he asked proudly, and slightly conspiratorially, as if he were letting me in on a secret. "See there? It's all in this book."

∽

Conner's workshop was in an old, white-painted and peeling schoolhouse that he bought, disassembled, and rebuilt behind his house. As the door creaked open, it took my eyes a moment to adjust to the dim light coming in from the side windows. Straight ahead, I could see a large, black cast-iron wood stove. To the right, the walls were painted blue, and there were stacks of wood of various sizes, from rough cut planks that looked like they had come directly from a tree to smaller, smooth pieces closer to violin size. These were stacked like library books on rough-hewn wooden shelves. There must have been enough wood in that storehouse to create dozens of instruments.

"I like to joke that I have plenty of firewood here," he said, laughing. "In case I need it."

I laughed with him, feeling that uneasy and humorous tension between just plain old wood and wood made special by its destination as a musical instrument. He picked up a plank of smooth curly red maple and showed it to me.

"This is my most valuable wood," he said. "See the knots, the design in that wood? It comes from struggle, from fighting the elements. Curly wood is wood with a defect, wood that's had to suffer to get where it is. It's beautiful wood, ain't it? It's what I make the backs from."

I looked at the wood, admiring its random designs and patterns drawn from struggle and hardship.

The workshop had screened windows looking out over tall, green vines and bushes, and a workbench and a stool that stood like a throne in the middle of an ordered chaos. Items filled every possible space on the workbench: a blue drill, pieces of wood, a vice, wood-handled scrapers and knives, scroll-shaped metal templates, a white ceramic mortar and pestle, a can of WD-40, a box of Band-Aids, halved plastic milk cartons filled with mysterious brown substances, a hot plate with a pan holding an old jar and a wooden spoon. On the wall hung rolls of tape, funnels, filters. An unvarnished violin dangled from the ceiling beneath skylights. In the midst of the cacophony of tools and wood wafted a complicated smell made up of varnish, dust, and the sharp, sweet scent of raw wood.

"The sound of the fiddle, it all has to do with the wood that it's made from," he explained. "The cells, the sap tubes, they all create the instrument's voice. My method, which is secret, keeps those sap tubes open so they can transmit and amplify the music."

I nodded, thinking as he talked about how intimately connected to the natural world was the violin. The wood, the horsehair bow, the rosin made from the sap of trees, the catgut traditionally used in the strings: all of it is drawn directly from the wilderness.

"This is my sanity here," he said, sweeping his arms and eyes across his shop. At first glance it looked like any other cluttered wood shop, with its saws and tools and dust. But as my eyes adjusted to the light streaming in through the Plexiglas skylights, I looked closely and saw a half-carved scroll among the tools, a nearly complete violin hanging above me, and more diagrams and books about violin design scattered on a nearby table.

He joked that his wife Ilene threatened to clean up his mess, but he said in fact he knew exactly where everything was.

"See, I got a place for everything," he said, picking up a wood gouge and putting it on the shelf. "This goes here, and this goes right there."

He sat on the stool, looking slightly flustered in the midst of his tools, as if he weren't sure where to begin.

Conner picked up a piece of red maple carved into the rough shape of the back of a violin and showed me how he whittled away the sides, the middle, measuring it as he went to see that his thicknesses are correct. We went through his shop like this, jumping from step to step, sometimes forward, sometimes backward. He had too much to tell me and not enough time. As he talked, I tried to piece together how he made fiddles from start to finish.

He said he begins with lengths of red maple and spruce, which he whittles down into rough fiddle shapes: the front, with its f-holes; the back, with its many different thicknesses to help channel the sound; the sides; the neck. He makes the back and sides and neck from curly maple, which gives the instrument the typical flared finish. The top is made from spruce, and the fingerboard and pegs are made from ebony.

Since he was a young boy, Conner said, he had honed his skills as a woodcarver, whittling pieces of wood with a little pocket-knife into tops, guns, gravel-shooters, and other toys. His mom died when he was ten years old, and his father didn't earn much money, so if young Arthur wanted toys, he had to make them. Now he uses those skills to carve the wood of fiddles. He focuses much of his artistic efforts on the scroll, which often becomes his trademark ram or cougar head. He assembles the pieces, shaping them and gluing them together, adding the fingerboard and pegs. After he finishes the body of the violin, he coats the instrument with a mixture of borax and lye, which he makes by running water through ashes in an upside down plastic container on his wall. He learned about this mixture from *The Secrets of Stradivari*, and he told me that it kills any bugs that threaten to eat the wood and cleans out the sap from the wood tubes—giving the violin its resonance.

Conner then coats the wood with tempera, a sealant made from egg whites, and varnishes it with a homemade mixture made from bee propolis, a substance produced by bees to seal their hives. According to *The Secrets of Stradivari,* this same substance was used by early Italian violin makers to seal the wood. Popular stories regarding Stradivarius violins suggest that their exquisite sound comes in part from his secret varnish formula. Although some scientific analysis of the varnish on Stradivarius violins has indicated that it's not much different from basic furniture varnishes of the time, the stories have real power for violinists and violin makers alike. Conner was thus particularly proud of his special propolis varnish recipe, which his beekeeping neighbor, Danny, made for him. Danny's a chemist by profession, and he created a secret recipe just for Conner, mixing the sticky substance bees produce to seal their wooden hives with other chemicals. Conner said that he didn't know the precise ingredients in this mixture, but he trusted Danny's recipe.

"What's in it, besides bee propolis?" I asked.

He eyed me carefully. "Think you could tell if you smelled it?"

I shrugged. "I guess I'd have to try."

He unplugged a small glass container holding dark brownish green liquid, and let me smell. I said it smelled like beeswax, and mint, and wood sap, and maybe turpentine. It smelled like something else that I didn't tell him, though. Somehow, it smelled faintly like the Blue Ridge Mountains.

∽◯

As the late afternoon light stretched across the green hills and woods, we went back to his house.

"Thanks so much for your time," I said.

"Wait a minute," he said. "You're not going anywhere yet."

He pulled out a case containing a set of his fiddles, one with five strings, and one with four. He handed me the four-string and took the five-string himself.

"It's time to play some fiddle," he said, smiling. "Show me what you can do."

Once again I froze, trying to remember some of the songs I'd been learning. I started playing a halfhearted rendition of "Ida Red," with its simple droning double-stops that I'd started learning with Angela.

Conner shook his head.

"I see you're trying to play old-time fiddle," he said. "But you know, that's not the way it's done. It's all in the timing. And the foot tapping. Can you tap your foot?"

As I began to tap, he belted out a soft and fast old-time version of a folk tune called "Eighth of January," which he said was about the Battle of New Orleans. He bowed in quick motions, back and forth, in a distinctive old-time way that I'd heard on recordings but couldn't quite figure out how to imitate. I tried to play along, but my tone sounded all wrong, too melodic, like the tone of a classical violinist. As he played the tune over and over, though, I began to get the hang of it a little, began to sense how the notes fit together in a pattern unlike any classical violin piece, began to understand how to make the continual droning sound of old-time fiddle without simply sounding weak. He was right; it was all in the timing, and in the foot tapping. It might have had something to do with the way he held the bow and the instrument, too, though I couldn't quite tell. He played a few other songs, such as "Alabama Girls" and "Rabbit Sittin' in the Cornfence," as well as a strange version of "Greensleeves" that was, as best as I could tell, in C major. Mostly, I listened, trying to join in as I could.

"Well, you keep practicing," he said, eyeing me skeptically and taking the fiddle from my hands. The ebony eyes of the fiddle's ram's head seemed hard and inscrutable. "You'll get there."

I have to admit, I'd been hoping he'd like my playing. He'd told me when I arrived, after all, that when good fiddlers visit him, they might leave with a fiddle. I'd been thinking I might be leaving with an instrument, but as I looked at him, I knew I wouldn't.

"Yeah, I'll keep trying," I said.

"That's how you do it," he said, laughing his grizzly laugh as he put both fiddles away in their double case, carefully nestling the rams' head scrolls in their places. "That's how you do it."

Chapter 4

A Brief History of the Fiddle

The history of the violin and its family is one of travel, movement, trade, and evolution. One of the basic ancestors of the violin is the lute, a plucked, string instrument that originated with the *ud*, or *oud*, which Arabs had introduced to Europe during their conquest and occupation of Spain beginning in the eighth century. From this instrument, Europeans developed the lute, a pear-shaped wooden instrument held much like the modern-day guitar, with six sets of plucked strings, in the early Middle Ages.

The moment a musician first picked up a bow and used it on strings is lost to history. As Kathleen Schlesinger argues in her 1914 book, *The Precursors of the Violin Family*, "The origin of the violin family is obscure, and it is only by conjectures, analogies, and inferences that we are able to proceed in tracing the instrument." Because of the resemblance of the violin's bow to a hunting bow, however, one theory is that its ancestors were invented by hunters. Walter Kolneder argues in his *Amadeus Book of the Violin: Construction, History, and Music* that "if in the violin's prehistory we wanted to include all instruments that had any of its characteristics, we would have to go back to primitive man. As he plucked the string of his hunting bow he might have become aware of a musical sound."

Many theories of the origins of the violin point to Asia, where various bowed instruments had been played for centuries. One of the possible ancestors of the violin is the Mongolian *morin khuur*. Other possible ancestors include the *rebab*, a northern Indian instrument played with a bow, and the *rebec*, a bowed Asian instrument with three strings tuned in fifths that was played throughout the Byzantine Empire. After years of occupations and trade between Byzantium and Italy, Spain, and France, bowed instruments like the *morin khuur, rebab,* and *rebec* probably made their way into the hands of Europeans. Furthermore, as these Asian bowed instruments came in contact with the lute, many different forms of bowed wooden instruments spread across Europe. One early European instrument to use bows was the *crwth*, which was used by bards to accompany songs and stories in Ireland, Wales, and northern France. Another instrument, the *fidl*, from the Latin *fidula*, was a bowed wooden instrument held on the left shoulder. These early bowed European instruments eventually evolved into instruments more like the modern-day violin.

The violin, in short, had a messy birth. There wasn't one first violin, but rather many hybrid instruments that combined, grew, and evolved in the hands of woodworkers, luthiers, and musicians. It grew out of multiple cultures, in many different dusty, cluttered workshops. The history of the violin is a practical history, an artistic history, a history of thought, creation, and evolution.

All of the violin's possible ancestors, both Asian and European, were folk instruments, played by a single player for a small
group of people. In Europe, however, demand had arisen for
a louder, more powerful instrument. Renaissance courts and
other performance venues began to assemble groups of string
players who could play music with more force than a single fiddler. They needed sound. And so luthiers, the name for lute
makers that eventually came to refer to any stringed instrument makers, fiddled with size and structure to create a series
of louder performance instruments with a greater range of tone
and sound, developing a new family of instruments, including
the low-voiced *viola da gamba* and the higher-voiced *viola da bracchio*,
both recent close cousins of the modern-day violin.

Sometime before 1500, it's likely that a luthier made a so-
prano *viola da bracchio* that sounded much like a violin, but there
are no exact records of that fact, and no agreement among music
historians about who did it first. Some historians claim that
Leonardo da Vinci worked out one of the first designs; others
credit a luthier named Giovanni Cellini. Still others suggest
that the mathematician Niccolò Tartaglia was responsible. Probably, however, many luthiers worked simultaneously in the late
fifteenth and early sixteenth centuries to create new, different,
and continually evolving instruments.

In the mid-sixteenth century, several famous Italian makers
invented and perfected instruments that came to be known as
true violins. The Amati family of Cremona and Bertolotti family of Brescia were the most famous of these, and Nicolò Amati
taught one of the most famous violin makers of all: Antonio
Stradivari. Born around 1644, Stradivari eventually set up his
own shop in Cremona. At first he imitated the violins of his
mentor, but then he began to experiment with measurements,

thicknesses, scroll styles, and sizes. It took him months to build each instrument, toiling away in his cluttered workshop, and as he perfected his art, his violins began to sound fuller, richer, and more melodic than any that had come before.

According to some theories, Stradivari's measurements and design for the instrument came as close as possible to perfect. He and his shop made the finest, most well-known instruments from 1698 to 1725, and these instruments soon became prized above all other violins. In fact, they were so prized, and so expensive, that luthiers across Europe began to copy Strads. Later, violins made by seventeenth- and eighteenth-century master luthiers like Jacob Stainer and Josephus Guarnerius were also fair game for copyists. Many claimed to build exact replicas of the violins of these top luthiers, or they simply put labels in their instruments that falsely claimed them to be originals.

Even as violin workshops across Europe tried to duplicate the measurements of Stradivari's instruments, selling these cheap copies to a growing middle class of performers and folk musicians, many luthiers, including Stradivari himself, actually experimented with various forms, sizes, and types of wood and inlays, creating a number of strange, curious, and unusual violins. Stradivari, in other words, would be the last one to have claimed to have reached perfection.

Those who have a more fiddle-oriented approach to the world understand this experimentation instinctively. The violin's many grandparents, uncles, and cousins and step-siblings form a ragged, adaptable, flexible, always-evolving musical family that did whatever it needed to survive, and it continues to evolve.

Those with a more violin-oriented perspective, though, tend to consider the four-stringed, bowed instrument to have been perfected as much as possible by the early seventeenth century.

The division between fiddles and violins is also rooted in different styles of playing. During the Renaissance, a split grew between high and low musical forms, between performance ensembles meant to entertain courts, kings, and concertgoers, and playing by folk musicians, who could be just about anyone who had an instrument and continued the music and dance traditions stretching back for centuries.

Most histories of the violin tell the history of *high violin:* the Stradivari and Guarneri violins, the players who performed on them in churches and courts and concerts, and composers like Vivaldi, Bach, Mozart, and Beethoven, who brought the art of the violin to higher and higher levels.

Yet at the same time, a lot of *fiddle* playing went on in taverns, on streets, and at dances for people who never went to noblemen's courts, fancy churches, or sit-down concerts. These lively folk traditions developed simultaneously and mostly surreptitiously beneath the other, more visible, history of classical music.

Because of their portability, violins were popular with folk musicians across Europe, and each region evolved its own particular form of fiddle music. Ireland, Scotland, England, Wales, France, Italy, Spain, Hungary, Romania, Poland, Germany, and Greece all had their own distinct fiddle traditions, which kept alive folk tunes passed down for centuries. Fiddles and fiddle tunes came to America on boats with immigrants from all of these countries, who hit the shores of this land and took their fiddling to Appalachian hollows, urban brownstones, and Southern backwaters. Each immigrant who brought a fiddle also brought an entire tradition of music and dance. And in the evenings in a shack, cabin, tenement apartment, or tent, a family's fiddler would pull out the instrument; kick back in the moonlight, gaslight, or firelight; and set out to play a tune.

Chapter 5

The Violin Shop

I opened the door to the Loft Violin Shop in Columbus, and a small bell jangled, announcing my entry. Coming inside the cool shop from the hot, humid summer day, I saw violins propped up in a glass case, a large string bass leaning against the corner, a bulletin board announcing violin lessons and bands for hire, a collection of electronic equipment and amps, and an electric violin propped up on a stand. I smelled a wonderful combination of wood and varnish in the air, and I felt, suddenly, like I had come home.

I wandered up to the front desk, and David Schlub, the shop's owner and founder, introduced himself. He wore a tan, leather work apron, and beneath that, jeans and a polo shirt. He looked like a cross between an eighteenth-century German luthier and a Cleveland Indians fan. He greeted me, and I told him I wanted to learn more about violins.

"Well, you've come to the right place," he said. "What do you want to know?"

"I don't know," I said, because I really didn't know exactly *what*

I wanted to know. I just wanted to *be* there, to absorb something of the essence of violins, to meet other violinists or, better yet, fiddlers. "Maybe I'll just hang around the shop for a while."

He shrugged, bemused. "Suit yourself," he said, eyeing me curiously. "Would you like a tour?"

"I'd love one," I said, barely able to contain my excitement.

He took me around back, past rows of hanging violins and cellos, into the bowels of the building, where luthiers were bent over instruments, carefully making repairs. One thirty-something luthier told me he played electric fiddle in a rock band in his spare time; another showed me a tiny hole in an old violin where a small woodworm had burrowed in.

"They can live for years in an instrument," he said. "Gradually they destroy the wood."

Schlub said they didn't make violins at the shop; mostly, they did repairs, and a large part of their business was working on school instruments.

As we walked around the shop, I asked Schlub what he thought about fiddles versus violins. Was there a difference between these instruments?

"The violin is a very exact, very precise instrument," he said, his tone itself exact and precise. "Fiddle makers do all sorts of things unacceptable to true violin makers—they round the corners; they use different finishes; they alter the number of strings or the width or length of the instrument . . ."

"Or put rams' heads on the scrolls?" I asked, thinking of Conner.

"Or that," he said.

I'd always loved violin shops, ever since my parents took me when I was in high school to Studio City Music on Ventura Boulevard to get my own violin. It was a small, narrow, dark shop, with rows of boxes on the wall holding violins. Along the side stretched a counter covered with books and papers, and the muffled sounds of customers trying out instruments in the back rooms filled the shop.

The old man behind the counter had ruffled hair and wrinkled skin.

"Can I help you?" he asked, looking at my mom, my dad, Ann, and me as we filed into the shop from the hot, frantic street outside.

"Yes, we're looking for a violin," my dad said proudly, looking over at me. "For my daughter."

A Holocaust survivor from a part-Jewish Hungarian family, my father was proud to be able to buy his daughter a violin. His pride embarrassed me, though, as did his excitement, his idea that I would find the best, most perfect violin, or at least the best one at the best price.

"Oh, are you?" the man said, eyeing me. "And what kind of violin are *you* looking for?"

I shrugged. "I don't know," I said. "I'm not sure."

"What price range?" the man, apparently unimpressed by me, asked my father.

"I'd like to keep it under a thousand," my dad half-whispered, as if I couldn't hear. It was more than my parents had ever spent on me in one go, so hearing my dad talk about such a large amount of money subdued me a bit, made me quietly grateful.

"Sure, sure, sure," the man said impatiently, and he walked out from behind his desk and went to the back. We dutifully followed him through a narrow, dusty hallway. He went into one room, where he pulled first one violin, then another, then another down from their boxes on the wall.

"Try these," he said, motioning for me to take them into a little room on the other side of the hallway. My parents helped me to carry the violins in, and then I stood there, feeling awkward, picking up the first one. My dad watched expectantly.

"I need to be alone," I said, thinking that was the way one tried out a violin. Alone with one's music. In fact, though, I didn't have a clue about what to do, how to tell the difference between one violin and another. I didn't even have any music with me, and I knew very little music by heart.

"Okay," my dad said. My little sister Ann looked at me and at the violins, her dark eyes big with expectancy and pride. "We'll just be out here in front. Let us know if you need something."

I played the first few measures of a Bach sonata, the only one I could remember, on the first violin I picked up. It sounded heavenly, so much richer, fuller, and more musical than my rental violin. Then I tried the next, and the next, and they all sounded lovely, so much so that I began to feel overwhelmed, in over my head, as if I were a fraud. Finally, after trying one after another, I picked one that I'd returned to several times, marveling at its deep, rich sound, its reddish color. I looked inside it through the f-hole and saw a label that said it was a Lyon & Healy student violin, crafted in 1910. Lyon & Healy, I'd learn later, was a Chicago company specializing in harp making. During the late nineteenth and early twentieth centuries, it also imported antique and new violins from European violin makers and resold them to middle-class American consumers. In 1910, my violin, a midrange student model, would have sold for about $50.

"That's the one you want?" the man asked, and suddenly I worried that I'd made the wrong choice.

"Um, yes," I stammered. "I like that one."

He nodded, studying the shiny reddish violin in his hands, the one with the deep sound and wide body, and then looking carefully at me, my mother, my father, and then back at me.

"It's a fine violin," he said. "I think you'll like it."

He packed it up for me in its original scuffed leather case, nestling the violin in the plush gold velvet lining, and zipping it in. My mom wrote a check for $750, and we left the shop, the door closing behind us with a soft swoosh. We went back out into hot, smoggy L.A., got in our little Toyota sedan, and headed north on the freeway. I held my new violin, a violin I would grow to love over the coming years as an extension of myself, as a friend and companion, on my lap all the way home.

At the Loft that afternoon, after we'd toured the workshop, David looked at me expectantly. "I suppose you want to look at some of our violins?" he said.

I hadn't really thought about it, but as soon as he said it I knew I did.

"Sure," I said.

We walked down to a dark, muffled room at the end of the hall, with a large glass case where different violins were propped on little holders. He pulled one out and handed it to me. "Try this one," he said.

Suddenly having a flashback to that moment in Studio City Music, and feeling as much of an impostor as I did then, I took the violin from him, holding it gingerly as if I'd never held one before. He gave me a bow, and I held the instrument up onto my shoulder. It was a glossy, light brown violin, and when I drew the bow across the strings, it had a haunting, beautiful voice. I tentatively played a C scale, and then a little Bach, a little Mozart. The instrument sang under my fingers, under my bow. The sound reverberated through the little room.

"It really is a beautiful instrument," I said.

"Yes," David said. "It's made by an excellent luthier out in Pennsylvania. We always try to stock one or two of his violins."

"How much does it cost?" I said, thinking it must be worth at least a thousand or two, and remembering that moment my mom wrote out the $750 check for my violin.

David took it from me, examined it for a moment. "This one, I believe, is twenty-five thousand dollars."

$25,000? And he'd let me *play* it?

"Uh, wow," I stammered, happy I was no longer holding it. "That's a lot."

David shrugged.

"Eh," he said. "It's middle range. Goes up a lot from there, you know." He smiled, and I edged toward the door, almost afraid of the case of instruments beckoning me from under glass.

"I guess I need to be going now," I said, backing slowly away from David, away from the violins, as if I were afraid they'd hurt me if I made any sudden movements.

"Okay," he said guardedly, still not sure, perhaps, of my motives. He walked me out to the front; I thanked him for showing me around his shop.

"Sure, come back to listen anytime," he said, smiling. "Have you met Charlene?" he asked.

The woman at the front counter looked over at us and held out her hand.

"Nice to meet you," she said.

"Thanks," I said.

David half waved at me and walked back to the workshop. Char-lene was talking to a fifty-something man with a wide girth and a pleasant demeanor, a violin case propped against his leg. I stood there for a moment, half in and half out of their conversation.

"So you're teaching at the festival again this year?" he asked her.

"Sure am," she said.

"What festival?" I asked, trying not to seem like I was butt-ing in.

"The Dublin Irish Festival," she said. "I play Irish fiddle."

She handed me a brochure and encouraged me to sign up.

"I teach the beginner's class," she said.

"That's great," I said. "Thanks. I play violin, but I'm really trying to learn more about fiddle."

The man laughed. "You want to know the difference between a violin and a fiddle?" he said, winking, his eyes glinting.

"Sure," I said.

"The fiddle's the one with the red neck!"

He laughed heartily, and Charlene and I joined in.

"That's good," I said. "So you're a fiddler, too?"

"Oh, of a sort," he said.

He told me that he played in the West Virginia Symphony and taught in the music program for Charleston's schools. But his real love, he said, was Scottish fiddle, and he competed regularly in various contests, including one coming up in September at the Highland Games in Pennsylvania. I nodded, not wanting to seem stupid, but not having a clue what the Highland Games were. It seemed an odd name, something more apt for an athletic event than for anything that had to do with fiddling.

"The Highland Games?" I asked.

"Sure, they're a lot of fun," he said. "Calum MacKinnon's going to be there this year as workshop leader and judge. Come on out to it; you'll enjoy it."

Murray gave me his card, which read "Darrell Murray, Violinist—Violist," listed his address in Charleston, West Virginia, and had a little cartoon graphic of a brown violin, smiling and holding its own bow in a playing position.

"Thanks," I said. "Maybe I'll look you up."

"You do that," he said good-naturedly. "I'd love to hear from you."

"I guess I have to go," I said, happy to have met a couple of real-life fiddlers. "I'll try to catch your workshop, Charlene."

"Sure thing," she said. "Hope to see you there."

She and Darrell waved and smiled as I went out the front door, the little bells jangling as I pushed the door open and let it swing shut behind me. I stepped out of the shop's magical, rarified, otherworldly atmosphere and back into the hot, humid summer day in Columbus.

Chapter 6

Body and Voice

Everything about the violin's body is designed to create, shape, and amplify the instrument's voice. This voice is one of vibrations, coming from the moment when the strings come into contact with the bow. The vibrations produced by this meeting are then amplified by the structure of the instrument's wooden form.

The natural acoustic properties of wood amplify sound vibrations. Choosing wood, therefore, has always been a top priority for luthiers. From the beginning, though, this choice was as much an art as a science. Kolneder notes: "Legend has it that Nicolo Amati and Jacob Stainer would walk through the woods during thunderstorms, on the lookout for trees hit by lightning. As the tree crashed to the ground, the sound it made told them whether it was suitable for violin making." There's a sense of poetry in this legend, based as it is on two strikingly different kinds of sound: a tree crashing to the forest floor and an instrument capturing the vibrations of strings. Yet it's a fitting stretch of the imagination, in a craft that relies as much on imagination as it does on scientific proof.

In the early days of violin making, the tops were typically made from the wood of trees common in the European landscape: red fir, hazel fir, silver fir, and white fir. Once violin making came to America, the wood choice changed to the more common spruce. The backs of violins have been, for centuries, made from various types of maple, both in Europe and America.

Early on, luthiers determined that the older and drier the wood, the better, since old wood is more stable, predictable, and it has better acoustics than young, fresh, and damp wood. The wood used for violin making is aged, therefore, sometimes for many decades. For the same reason, the wood for violin making is taken from the hardest part of the tree, as Harvey Green notes in his *Wood: Craft, Culture, History:* "The trees must be more than twice the width of the back to be useful, since the pith and sapwood are normally discarded." Many luthiers think that the curly, or distressed, maple often used for the back creates a more complicated sound than wood with straight veins, as Conner had told me that day in his workshop. Green concurs that this, in fact, might be true: "It does seem reasonable to argue that wave motions will perhaps achieve a color and depth when encountering wood with striations."

In addition to the wood itself, the violin's sound also comes from the shaping, carving, and manipulation of the wood. The shape of the violin's body creates a sound box, an enclosed space that amplifies, mixes, and transmits sound produced by the strings and bow. Measurements for the wood and its thickness on the back and front plates have been handed down for centuries, and the vibrations created by the wood are dependent on the precision of the luthier's woodworking. Inside the violin, there is a bass bar, or a long strip of wood, attached to the top plate directly parallel to the violin's deepest string, the G string. This bar helps to amplify the bass notes, or the lower frequency notes. A small circular piece of wood called a sound post attaches the front plate to the back, transmitting vibrations from one to the other and mixing them together. The violin has two f-holes carved into the top plate, and these also amplify and transmit the vibrations from the sound box to the air.

The bow is also central to the violin's sound. Its stick is generally made out of Pernambuco wood, a variety of Brazil wood, and strung with long lengths of horsehair. Running the bow across strings sets up a series of vibrations, including transverse (perpendicular to the string) and longitudinal (parallel to the string). At the same time the strings vibrate axially, turning around on themselves. This nexus of vibrations is transmitted into the sound box through the bridge, sound post, bass bar, and other parts of the violin. The bow's interactions with the strings thus creates a heady mix of vibrations, going at first in all different directions, but eventually synthesizing into one voice.

The horsehair on bows traditionally comes from the tails of horses, usually from Siberia, Mongolia, Manchuria, Poland, and Argentina. As Mary VanClay notes in her article, "From Horse to Bow," which appeared in *Strings*, stallion hair is generally preferred, since "it is generally cleaner than that of mares, which tends to get hit with more urine spray." Bow makers also prefer hair from horses in northern climates, where it tends to grow stronger. The straighter the hair, the better, since straight hair provides a more consistent tone than twisted or kinky hair. Most violin bows use white hair, though some bass and cello bows are made with coarser black hair.

Rosin, or treated and processed tree sap, also contributes

to the violin's voice. Without rosin, the horsehair bow would have no bite to it, and it would create few, if any, vibrations in the strings. Rosin is made with pine or other tree sap, which is harvested, heated, and shaped into small cakes that are cooled, hardened, and wrapped in fabric. Some rosins even have gold flakes or other additives, which are thought to increase bite and deepen tone. Violinists run their bows across these green, brown, or clear gold cakes of rosin, putting a white powder onto the horsehair that will help the hair catch on the strings and set up their complex network of vibrations.

Early strings for both plucked and bowed instruments were traditionally made out of animal intestines, usually from sheep. This is where the term "catgut" comes from, though the guts were never from cats. European string makers tended to prefer sheep intestines, particularly those from wild and mountain sheep, since they were stronger and tore less easily than the intestines from domestic animals. These guts were cut from the body, dried, treated in alkaline substances or red wine, stretched, and twisted into varying thicknesses for varying pitches. Gut strings were difficult to keep tuned, though, and they also broke regularly. String makers experimented with other materials, including silk, and in the eighteenth century they had begun to develop a winding process, using copper, silver alloy, bronze, and aluminum wound around gut or other materials to stabilize and strengthen the strings. In the nineteenth century, steel strings were developed and experimented with, and while they didn't work so well for the lower strings, they are still often used for the violin's E string. Contemporary strings are rarely made from gut; rather, they are made from synthetic materials wound with metal.

All of these components come together to create that elusive entity: the instrument's voice. The science of the violin is a combination of the known and unknown, the quantifiable and the unquantifiable, technology and art. The violin's body, with its curved wood, its gut, its hair, is like a living body, crafted out of natural materials and sent into the world to live.

Chapter 7

Cuts, Rolls, and Audis
Learning Irish Fiddle in Dublin (Ohio)

Dublin, Ohio, is a suburb northwest of Columbus with a vague Irish heritage and a lot of money. I realized the lot-of-money part when, trying unsuccessfully one evening to find the Dublin Community Recreation Center, where my Introduction to Irish Fiddle workshop with fiddler Charlene Adzima would begin in about five minutes, I pulled into a car dealership called the Toy Barn so I could stop and look at the map.

Suddenly, I found myself navigating a sea of shiny Jaguars, BMWs, Audis, and Mercedes, all of which were, presumably, Dublin's toys. At first I worried about running into them, and then I worried that if I stopped, a salesman might approach me to see if I was ready to trade in my aging minivan for something, well, a little more *Dublin*.

I quickly pulled out of the lot and didn't look back.

After this narrow escape, I circled through Dublin, past roads blocked off for the upcoming Dublin Irish Festival. The Dublin Community Recreation Center was on Post Road, but orange cones blocked that road off and I could find no other entrance. Finally, at 6:29 p.m., one minute before the class would begin, I broke down and called the center, trying recklessly to drive with one hand and talk on my cell phone with the other.

"Oh, yeah, all the roads are blocked off for the festival," the woman on the other end told me. I could hear commotion behind her voice, apparently people rushing here and there to get to their Irish workshops of choice. "You need to come down Tara Road, and then left on Downpatrick."

Following her instructions, driving through toney, Irish-themed housing developments, I finally found the Recreation Center. My workshop was part of the Irish Music Academy, several days of classes preceding the annual Dublin Irish Festival. One of the biggest Irish festivals in the country, it features a long weekend of music, dance, workshops, Guinness, whiskey, and large, hot crowds eager for a taste of their real, imagined, or adopted Celtic ancestry.

The photocopied brochure Charlene had given me described all the festival's workshops: Beginning, Intermediate, and Advanced Irish Fiddle; Beginning and Advanced Irish Whistle; Sean Nos Singing; Beginning and Intermediate Bodhran; Button Accordion; Irish Language; Country Set Dancing. Looking through this wealth of workshops, I had finally found Charlene's class:

Introduction to Irish Fiddle

This class is for students who already know how to play the violin fairly well and would like to learn the basics of Irish traditional fiddling. This includes jigs, reels, and other dance music, basic ornamentation, learning tunes by ear, and how to find and play in an Irish session. Charlene

Adzima has been steeped in the Irish fiddling tradition for more than a decade, as well as being an outstanding classically trained player. She has toured nationally with the band Oisre and recently completed a solo CD.

And as I read it I knew: *I'm so there.* I'd called the Dublin Community Recreation Center right away and registered over the phone, giving my credit card number for the $50 fee.

That night I'd left the kids at home with their dad and headed into Columbus, eager to learn whatever I could at the workshop. They'd all become accustomed to Mom's obsession with fiddling by then, taking it in stride, letting me go. Even my husband seemed nonchalant about my leaving.

"See ya," he'd said as I went out to the garage to get in the van.

"Bye—be back late," I said.

"Yup," he said. And I left.

By then I'd thrown myself headlong into this fiddle journey. I still didn't really know what I was doing, and there was no way I could call myself a fiddler. But I had started down that road, and I wasn't turning back.

Dublin actually does have some vaguely Irish roots. The U.S. government had handed over two thousand acres along the Scioto River in the late eighteenth century to Revolutionary War lieutenant James Hill as payment for his military service. The Sells family purchased four hundred acres of this land in the early nineteenth century, and John Sells and his partner John Shields platted the village of Dublin, named after Shields's Irish birthplace, in 1810.

It had remained a sleepy, remote village far from the center of

Columbus until the 1970s, when the I-270 outerbelt stretched out and embraced it. Coupled with the arrival of several business headquarters, including Wendy's International and Ashland Chemical Company, as well as the building of the Muirfield Village Golf Club and residential community, Dublin's economy boomed. In 1987, when it surpassed ten thousand residents, it incorporated as a city, and it now has more than thirty-six thousand residents.

It also has lots of fancy cars, and they drive on streets called Tara Hill, Roscommon, Killarney, Emerald Park—a network of Irish-themed roadways threaded through green parks and well-kept sidewalks and comfortably large homes. The Irish theme, based on a partly real, partly imagined past, gives the suburb its sense of identity. On road signs and billboards and brochures throughout the city, you see its logo: a bright green shamrock. It's a place where kids wearing helmets ride their top-of-the-line bikes on bike paths. A place with a calm, cool, collected, middle class air. An enclave of manufactured Irish identity in a hazy spread of otherwise anonymous suburban sprawl.

The center turned out to be a large, impressive building with an even larger and more impressive schedule of activities and classes, as I'd see later in its newsletter: yoga, knitting, Reiki Level One training, weight training, Chinese classes, pottery, water gardening. You name it, the Dublin Community Recreation Center has it.

As I walked through the glass doors, I first noticed the renovations. "We're expanding to better serve you," announced a large sign propped on the dusty floor. To the right, I found my classroom, with a small sign taped on the door: Introduc-

TION TO IRISH FIDDLE. Charlene sat in a chair, her fiddle in hand, her light brown hair tied casually behind her head. When she saw me, a glimmer of recognition showed in her hazelnut-colored eyes.

"Hi," she said. "I know you. What's your name again?"

I told her, and she said, "Welcome, glad you could make it."

One other student was already there, a boy maybe about sixteen with a full head of dark hair. He sported a white T-shirt that read DUBLIN IRISH FESTIVAL accompanied by a large green shamrock.

"Hi," I said, suddenly feeling like a high school student myself.

"Hi," he said.

I put my case on the table and opened it, unzipping the blue cover and releasing the locks on the cracked and faded leather case, and unzipped the gold velvet inside to reveal my violin.

Charlene's workshop met in an all-purpose meeting room with beige carpet, watercolors of misty Dublin streets on the wall, and stacks of chairs and tables. I pulled up a comfortable, padded blue chair and sat by the young man in the Dublin Irish Festival T-shirt. I held my violin, waiting expectantly for my introduction to Irish fiddle. We sat and waited, and eventually a few other people came in: two women about my age, both of whom told the group they were stay-at-home moms, and two other teenagers. One of the teens was a skinny, earnest boy whose bow had strange, green horsehair; the other was a sullen young girl who had just started taking fiddle lessons with Charlene and scowled through most of the workshop.

"Okay, then," said Charlene. "I think we're all here now, so we can get started."

She instructed us to pull our chairs into a tight circle, in order to emulate the structure of a traditional Irish session. She told us that sessions are informal gatherings of Irish musicians in pubs, often including a fiddler, a bodhran, or Irish drum, player, a guitarist, a whistle player, and others. At a session, tune after traditional tune will be played, typically late into the night, the musicians egged on by each other and by the Guinness-drinking crowd around them. Ours was a peculiar, rather sterile little session in the Dublin Community Recreation Center, but it would have to do.

Charlene asked if we were all comfortable playing "Twinkle, Twinkle Little Star," and we all nodded unenthusiastically.

"It'll be a chance to warm up and practice playing by ear," she said, almost apologetically, perhaps seeing the disappointment in our eyes that we weren't starting with something *Irish*, but rather with this boring, simple tune we'd all learned as beginning violinists. The teenage girl frowned as we played, looking frustrated with her fingers and her instrument. It occurred to me that maybe she *hadn't* yet learned "Twinkle, Twinkle."

"Okay," Charlene said when we finished. "So you're all good players. Let's get started."

She told us that Irish music has *songs* and *tunes*: songs have words, and tunes don't. We'd be learning *tunes,* which was something I kept forgetting throughout the workshop.

"What song are we playing now?" I'd ask.

She'd look sharply at me. "Tune," she'd say. "We're playing *tunes.*"

Finally by the end I started to get it right. *Tunes.* We were playing *tunes.*

Charlene said she'd started playing violin, like me and most other violinists I'd ever met, with the Suzuki method. When her mom took up Irish dancing at the local YWCA, though, Charlene had fallen in love with Irish dance tunes and taught herself how to play them. Irish fiddle music, she told us, is mainly based on a variety of dance styles: jigs, reels, barn dances, set dances, waltzes, hornpipes, polkas. You might not ever hear, or play, exactly the same tune twice.

"Here's a jig you've all heard before," she said while her fingers belted out the tune, then again but this time slightly changed, and then again but faster. "You can kind of make it your own within the rules set up by the tradition."

Making a tune your own partly involves ornamentation. Charlene handed us a photocopied packet, pointing out the page on ornamentation, where she'd listed and defined some of the basic forms: slides, cuts, rolls, double-stops.

Slides, she'd written, involve playing the note below or above the actual note and sliding up or down in one bow stroke. Cuts are a way to play the same two notes in one bow stroke. To do a cut, you throw one of your fingers down on the string hard enough to stop, or cut, the vibration, even as the bow keeps moving. Rolls involve quickly going up, going down, and then landing on the original note.

"Rolls took me months to understand, and then years to get them sounding right," she admitted.

As we practiced each of these ornamentations, I began to realize that this wasn't going to be easy. Though she made it all seem so simple when she played, we were like toddlers learning our first words. We tried, and we worked at it. And we all understood what she meant: to do this, we'd have to practice. I guess I'd been hoping to attend this workshop and have Irish fiddle infused into me, like a magical serum, and that I'd go home with new skills to dazzle my friends and family.

But no, it would take work.

Damn.

⚬⚬

Ireland's early string instruments were primarily versions of the lyre, which were plucked, stringed instruments. Archaeological excavations have shown that bowed instruments began to make their way to Ireland sometime in the eleventh century. One medieval fiddle, for instance, with a bow made of dogwood and with an animal head carving at the tip, was found buried beneath a Dublin house in the eighteenth century.

By 1674, Richard Head wrote that Ireland had "in every field a fiddle." The fiddle, by that time closer to a standardized violin, was a cheap and popular instrument in the country, relatively easy to learn and to bring along to dances, weddings, and pub sessions. Along with Uilleann pipes and bodhrans, the fiddle had become one of Ireland's most popular folk instruments.

Most Irish fiddle is based on a variety of dance tunes, including reels, hornpipes, polkas, jigs, and slip jigs, but there are many different styles. The Donegal style from the northwest part of the country is fast, without a lot of ornamentation. The Sligo style is lighter and breezier, with lots of ornamentation. The Clare style is slower, with subtle ornaments, and the Cork and Kerry styles are more polka oriented.

Sessions are central to Irish fiddling. Sessions are gatherings at pubs in which fiddlers and other instrumentalists play through sets of different tunes. Sessions are integral to keeping

Irish fiddle traditions alive and passing down music, and they remain common both in Ireland and the United States.

With the great potato famine of 1845–1849, many Irish fiddlers emigrated to the United States, bringing their talents to pubs, bars, and minstrel shows in cities across the East Coast. In the early twentieth century, recordings of fiddle sessions by musicians like Michael Coleman brought Irish fiddle to the masses and helped to spark the popularity of Ceili bands, which keep the tradition of Irish fiddling alive today.

∽

The first tune Charlene taught us was an upbeat and fairly simple one called "Egan's Polka." She played it through, telling us to listen to the two parts and how they repeat.

"The good thing about Irish music is that you only have to learn parts, and then you repeat them," she said.

I listened, entranced by the lilting sound of her Irish fiddle. But this time, unlike when I watched Riverdance on PBS, I listened closely. And instead of just hearing the hum and flow of a beautiful foreign language, I heard the ornamentation, the slides and cuts and rolls. I also heard the two parts, how the A part repeated once, and the B part repeated once, and then the A part returned.

She also taught us "Shoe the Donkey," a Polish mazurka popular primarily in the northern counties of Ireland. I wanted to ask her how a Polish mazurka ended up in northern Ireland, but things moved too quickly, and we had too much to learn. Later, I'd read that mazurkas were common dance tunes in County Donegal. Though there's no consensus about how they arrived in northern Ireland, scholars hypothesize that mazurkas might have accompanied Polish immigrants or military regiments stationed in Ireland.

Charlene taught us the notes, phrasing, parts, and possible ornamentations for "Shoe the Donkey." She also taught us the dance that goes with the tune, and we awkwardly followed her around the room, imitating the distinctive skipping, hopping, and jumping involved in the tune's dance.

"It helps to play it if you know how the dance goes," Charlene said.

At the end of that first night, I asked Charlene if I could videotape her playing the tunes we'd learned, because I knew that as soon as I got home, I'd forget them entirely. She said I could, so I pulled out my new Canon PowerShot digital camera with video capability, a fortieth birthday present from my husband a few weeks before, and as she began to play, I hit RECORD.

At home the next morning, I plugged my camera into my computer, clicked on the video, and RealPlayer kicked into gear, with Charlene playing "Egan's Polka" and "Shoe the Donkey." I noodled along with her on my violin, trying over and over to capture something of the spirit, if not the exact ornamentation, of her fiddling. I spun around my office, playing through the two tunes, suddenly feeling very spry and Irish. I played them again and again, imagining green fields at night and cliffs and sea breezes and pubs and laughter and the clinking of pints of Guinness in the dark.

William came into my office and asked me what I was doing, and I played the tape of Charlene for him, and then my versions of the tunes.

He eyed me warily. I knew my family was wondering what was up with me. Why I was driving to Columbus for late-night workshops, why I was dancing around my office with my violin. But I didn't really know. I just knew that fiddling suddenly fascinated me. I was in love with it.

"Interesting," he said.

"It *is* interesting," I insisted. "Want to play along?"

"No, that's all right," he said.

"Really?" I asked.

"*Really*," he said, returning to his PlayStation FIFA '07 soccer game in the family room.

♋

The second night of our two-night workshop I pulled out my violin before class and ran through "Egan's Polka." As I played, Charlene walked in.

"Now play it so someone would want to dance to it," she said playful yet critical, with a quick-witted, mocking air about her.

Crestfallen, I realized that I didn't yet have what the night before she'd called "swing."

I tried again, but I knew I still didn't quite have it.

"It's okay," Charlene said. "You'll get it."

Then she picked up her fiddle and played the same tune, tapping her black boots back and forth, making a drum of the carpeted floor, and we could all hear the difference. Even the scowling, Gothic teenage girl across the circle from me smiled a little.

"You always want to play so your dancers want to dance," she told us.

I made a mental note: work on *swing*.

That night, she taught us a rather long and complicated piece: "John Kelly's Concertina Reel." This time, several of us had brought our video cameras. "You're all doing the video thing tonight," she said, self-consciously. "Ack!"

She began to play, tapping and swaying and ornamenting her way through the tune, and as she did so she became oblivious to our cameras. After she played it for us, she broke down its parts, had us memorize each one, showing us how she slipped various ornaments in and among the basic notes.

She talked with us that night about different settings of tunes. She said that settings happen when a fiddler hears a tune in a pub, for instance, likes it, and then goes home and tries to recreate it. The tune he recreates might barely resemble the one he heard originally, given the various tricks and turns of one's memory. But he goes back to the pub the next night and plays it, calling it by the same name as the tune he'd heard the night before. What he plays is called a new setting of that original tune.

Irish tunes, Charlene said, change constantly with the whims and styles of different fiddlers, and there's not one right way to play a tune. Sure, there's a style, and there are rules, but the main goal is to take a tune and make it your own.

As the class ended, she encouraged us to attend some Irish sessions around Columbus, including one she'd been trying to get started at a Starbucks in Dublin, and an Irish set dancing group that meets every other week in Worthington.

"The world of Irish fiddlers is pretty small," she told us. "And now you're a part of it."

As I navigated out of the green, well-kept neighborhoods of Dublin and onto I-270, I felt like I'd been in a special place where a small, sputtering flame of folk tradition had been kept alive for a couple of nights, hidden away in an anonymous and incongruously modern suburban recreation center.

Driving home on the freeway, I listened to the melodies of

"Egan's Polka," "Shoe the Donkey," and "John Kelly's Concertina Reel" echoing in my mind, and the rhythm of cars switching in and out of lanes seemed to copy the rhythm of those dances. Cuts, triplets, and rolls spun through my head, handed down from fiddler to fiddler, from smoky pub to smoky pub, and now from Charlene to me.

I couldn't wait to pull out my fiddle, play through those tunes, and work on making them my own. When I got home, my husband had already put the kids to bed and gone to sleep himself. I slipped downstairs to the basement and pulled out my violin, running quietly through the trills and runs of "John Kelly's Concertina Reel," trying not to wake up my family.

Chapter 8

Real Men Wear Skirts
Scottish Fiddle at the Highland Games

The day I drove to the Highland Games dawned bright and cool, a September morning beginning to feel a bit like fall. Once again, I kissed the kids good-bye, told my husband I'd be back sometime in the early evening, and hit the road. I had started to love my fiddle hunting, if only because it gave me the chance to take trips like this. An excuse to get out of the house, on the road, on my own. I'd spent years staying close to home, caring for my husband and kids, focused on making my family happy and stable. Now, suddenly, I was going on regular adventures, which felt freeing. And every time I went out there, I'd discovered something important. Something I could use. Something that would help me evolve into the future, whatever it might hold.

I brought a cup of coffee in the car with me and drove east toward Pennsylvania, past Wheeling and Pittsburgh on Interstate 70, and finally on and up to the Scottish-sounding "highlands" area of Pennsylvania's Allegheny Mountains. As I drove, I thought about my mom's Scottish, Scots-Irish, and German pioneer ancestors making this trek in the opposite direction, following the ruts of covered wagon trails, from Pennsylvania to California. I, on the other hand, followed the interstate and its endless lines of semitrucks on a pronounced upward and eastward climb, past maple forests with leaves just on the cusp of losing their summer green.

The games are held each fall in Idlewild Park, a recreational area founded in 1878 just outside of Ligonier, Pennsylvania. This would be the forty-ninth annual Highland Games, and I'd seen on the website that it would feature bagpipe contests, dog shows, and dances, as well as the Scottish fiddle workshops and contest. I'd decided not to bring my violin, since I wanted to spend time wandering around the festival itself and didn't want to have to worry about my violin sitting in the hot car after the workshop. At least, I thought, I could sit in on the workshop and see what it was all about. Then perhaps I'd catch some of the contest before I had to get back home in time to make dinner for my family.

A few days earlier, I'd pulled Darrell Murray's card out of my wallet and looked at the little cartoon violin, finally getting up the nerve to call him.

"Remember me?" I asked him when he answered the phone. "I met you at the Loft a while back?"

"Oh, yes, yes," he said, laughing. "The fiddler-wannabe. So what can I do for you?"

"Um, well," I stammered, trying to think of an excuse for having called him. "I'm thinking of going to the Highland Games, and I just wanted to find out a little more about them, and you, and Scottish fiddling."

"Oh, I can talk your ear off about that, if you let me," he said.

"That's fine," I said. "Go ahead."

Darrell talked about playing with the West Virginia Symphony and how he was part of a program with the symphony that had him teaching in the Charleston public schools one or two days a week. He'd grown up in Lancaster, Ohio, earning his B.A. in music education from Ohio University and his M.A. in violin performance from Cleveland State. His early musical background was mostly classical, though he said he did have a stint as a jazz violinist in college at OU in the 1970s, when one of his professors asked him to play in a jazz concert with the university's big band.

"I was thrown into it," he said, remembering those days. "But mostly I was entertaining myself."

After studying classical music in graduate school and getting the job at the West Virginia Symphony, Darrell said he had his first taste of fiddle music, by chance, on a tour bus with the symphony.

"One of my friends put a Mark O'Connor CD in, and I was totally blown away," he said. I wasn't sure who Mark O'Connor was, but later I'd look him up and realize he was a famous fiddler who'd started on the contest circuit and now focused on writing and recording new music and running fiddle workshops and camps.

Murray said he decided, right then and there, that he would learn fiddle. Something about the music called to him, beckoned to him, offered him something he wasn't getting in his everyday classical violin playing. So he began going to summer fiddle camps hosted by O'Connor outside of Nashville in 1996, and he discovered he loved fiddling.

"I had a marvelous time," he said of that first summer camp he attended. "It was actually overwhelming."

As he described all the different workshops he encountered

at O'Connor's camp—jazz, bluegrass, contest style, Texas swing, Scottish—I could hear a certain breathlessness in his tone. It was the same feeling I'd been having as I'd started to explore fiddle music. A sense of amazement at all the different styles, and the sense of endless possibility and permutation they promised.

Darrell said he'd been going to O'Connor's camp just about every summer since then, honing his skills and learning new techniques. Fiddling had become a hobby and a passion for him. He played in fiddle contests, and he'd begun teaching fiddle lessons. And, over time Scottish fiddle had become his real love.

"So are you actually Scottish?" I asked.

"Oh, sure," he said. "My mother's father's family came from Scotland. And my mother took him to Scotland once to visit the village where he grew up."

Fiddling, he said, had even begun to influence his work as a symphony musician, giving him new insight into the music, allowing him to hear things differently than before, and providing him with inspiration.

"Now in the orchestra I'm feeling fresher," he said. "As I'm playing Scottish fiddle, I start to hear more in the music, and I'm probably playing better."

Darrell said he likes to travel to Scottish fiddle contests and festivals, including the Highland Games in Pennsylvania. He said the contests give him a chance to try his hand at new things, meet new people, and just have fun.

"I don't take it too seriously," he said of the Scottish fiddle concert circuit. "If you don't let it destroy your psyche, it's fun."

I told him I'd be coming out to the games and looked forward to seeing him and hearing him play. He laughed a deep, slightly Scottish-sounding laugh.

"Just look for a man in a kilt," he said. "A kilt made of Murray tartan."

∽◦

As I entered Idlewild Park, I navigated the van by the guard shack, drove past signs and bagpipers and other cars, and parked in a dirt lot. Getting out with my camera and notebook, I made my way past closed rides and boarded-up buildings. The park was closed for the season, and the Scottish Americans and their Highland Games had it all to themselves for the weekend. Fragments of bagpipe music wafted on the cool morning air, reminding me of early mornings at Camp Arrowbear, a music camp in the southern California mountains that I attended for a few years in junior high and high school. Each morning, after the trumpet sounded reveille, I shivered into jeans, ate pancakes in the mess hall, brushed my teeth in frigid mountain water, and headed for the practice tent. There the camp orchestra would warm up at 8 a.m., while the sound of music floated, along with the smell of pancakes, between pine trees and cabins.

That morning in western Pennsylvania was right on the border between summer and fall, and the closed rides seemed forlorn, a strange contrast to the lively Scottish festival brewing around them. A few people were arriving at the same time as me, dressed in their Scottish best and studying the maps they'd printed out from the festival's website.

"Are all the rides closed?" a young girl asked her kilted dad as they walked around the park waiting for the festivities to begin. "Even the Spider?"

"Even the Spider," he said.

Finally I found the fiddle gazebo, a small, circular wooden

structure where Calum MacKinnon, a soft-spoken, gray-haired man with a lilting Scottish accent, was already holding court for his 9 a.m. beginning fiddle class. The fiddle gazebo was sandwiched between the Howler, the Spider, and a closed concession stand called the Feedbox.

Everything had an end-of-the-season air about it. MacKinnon, wearing a green and yellow tartan kilt with a leather, silver-buckled belt and a soft-looking green short-sleeve shirt, focused in the early part of the workshop on beginning skills, by teaching the group several tunes and Scottish ornamentations. I didn't want to disrupt the class, so I hovered around the gazebo in the bushes, using the video function on my camera to film pieces of the workshop, feeling a bit like a spy. I saw Darrell Murray leaning against the railing of the gazebo, decked out in a kilt made of green, blue, black, and red Murray tartan, a loose white cotton shirt, a black felt cap, and long black socks. I waved at him, and he smiled, holding his fiddle up in greeting. The rest of the class was a mix of adults and children, some of whom wore kilts, scarves, and skirts in preparation for the contest, which required participants to dress in traditional Scottish garb. They all seemed intent on listening to MacKinnon, trying to grasp whatever crumbs of Scottish wisdom they could.

"Scottish music has pitch-driven dynamics," MacKinnon said to the group. For a split second, he glanced out quizzically at me, where I stood with my notebook and camera in the bushes. "As you go up in pitch, you go up in dynamics."

He played a wisp of a tune, "The Deathchair Tree," I thought he said, though I found out later it's called "The Duchess Tree." I had a hard time hearing his soft voice from my awkward vantage point. Sometimes his voice faded away, and I didn't have any idea what he'd just said. Like his voice, the tune he played for the group sounded plaintive and remote, as if he were channeling music from faraway highlands.

He went over snaps and reverse snaps, which are the short/long, long/short bowing patterns common to Scottish music. He showed how they're all a matter of bow speed, of slowing down and speeding up.

"These are not golden rules," said MacKinnon, softly, almost conspiratorially. "They're just broad guidelines."

He guided the workshop participants gently through the tune, saying, "This bar has four reverse snaps in it. The one that's got a dot on it increases the value by fifty percent, and if it doesn't have a dot that decreases its value by fifty percent."

He taught the group a *strathspey*, which is a snap-filled dance tune in 4/4, named after the Strathspey region in Scotland. He said that it's an up-and-down dance tune good for Highland dancing, which is vertically oriented. Scottish country dancing, on the other hand, he said, is more horizontal.

"This is really highland dancing stuff," he said, launching with vigor into the strathspey.

Scottish fiddling, like Irish, has its roots in dance music. It has its reels, its jigs, and its airs, but they have a particularly Scottish flavor. Much Scottish fiddling imitates the sound of bagpipes, and some of the common ornamentations like snaps make the fiddle sound like bagpipes.

Each part of Scotland, from the Shetlands to the west coast to the mainland, has its own fiddling style. Some of the best Scottish fiddling has actually been developed over the past hundred years in Cape Breton, Nova Scotia, where Scottish immigrants settled and perfected their art.

Scottish, and Scots-Irish, fiddlers also made their way into the Appalachian mountains, bringing their tunes with them into the valleys and remote towns in this region. Many of the sixteenth- and seventeenth-century tunes from Scotland, with their princes and princesses, their faeries, their dead maidens, soon became traditionally American tunes.

To study Scottish fiddling, then, is to study the roots of American roots music: to look back in time and to trace a path of adaptation common to all folk fiddle styles.

The group, about fifteen adults and a few kids, sat in the small, shaded gazebo, draped with vines and covered with peeling gray paint. Families walked by, the fathers and children and even some babies clad in kilts made from the family's traditional tartan pattern, the mothers dressed in skirts and sashes in the same fabric. One father I saw walked by in a black tank top and a red and black kilt. His daughter was in a red tartan dress, the mother in a white blouse and tartan sash.

In the background, I caught pieces of bagpipe tunes and a keyboard playing, readying itself for dancers. The late season maple trees shading the pavilion sighed in the wind, and the sun began to peek through the clouds and mist that had been shrouding the sky. There in the bushes outside the pavilion, I thought: *Why didn't I bring my violin?* And then, *Why didn't I bring my sunblock?* I sat on a rock by a trash can, next to a yew bush, so I could hear MacKinnon's soft voice and instructions, but at the same time stay out of his way, and out of his line of sight.

While the workshop progressed, a marching band passed with bagpipes blaring, some of the marchers carrying rifles, all of them wearing red coats. MacKinnon said good-naturedly to workshop, "Did you bring the rifle?" The workshop participants laughed as MacKinnon started playing along with the passing charge, his fiddle joining the band's lilting tune.

"So, where were we?" he said when the band finally passed, crossing the wooden bridge nearby and heading out to some distant field. "Ah, yes, there are two ways to do snaps: snap bowing and finger snaps."

He showed the class how to do these, before progressing on to mordants and grace notes, phrasing and melodies, double-stops and keys.

"All of these little things, when they all add up together, finish up to a very nice piece of music," he said.

One of the main things he emphasized in the workshop was the importance of thinking ahead, of planning for the next transition, the next tune.

"As you get into the last two or three bars of a tune or a part of a tune, you need to start thinking about what's coming ahead," he said. "This is something you've got to learn how to do."

As he said that, I thought: *He's right. I need to think about what I'm going to do next.*

∽∾

During a break, I talked for a few minutes with MacKinnon. He told me that he grew up in Scotland, playing classical violin and fiddle since he was eight years old. After he immigrated to the United States in 1966, when he was twenty-seven, he moved first to Arizona and then to Seattle, where he got a job as an aeronautical engineer with Boeing. He'd kept that job until he retired in 1999.

"I gave up Boeing for bowing," he said, laughing a lyrical, Scottish-accented laugh.

Since retirement, he had been teaching and leading work-shops, like the one that morning. Half-jokingly, I asked him what he thought of all this Scottish stuff, and he smiled.

"Well, you know," he said, with his thick Scottish drawl, wav-ing in the general direction of bagpipe bands, dance tents, and kilted fathers. "Some of these people are more Scottish than the Scots. Some of them go a little overboard, no? Like the blessing of the tartans—no one does that in Scotland. That's an Ameri-can tradition."

I nodded. I'd been wondering whether this kind of event was as much an exercise in nostalgia as in true historical or cultural recreation. It all seemed an invention, though a creative one, of a fanciful past. But at the same time, it was a creation of a new and innovative present.

As we stood there I noticed a thirty-something woman just kind of hanging out, listening to my conversation with MacKin-non. She had been in the workshop, and she seemed quiet and shy, though with a sharp, intelligent glint in her eyes. She intro-duced herself as Leigh Ann Hood, a school librarian from Fair-mont, West Virginia. A fiddler in mostly the old-time tradition, she said she was attending the workshop to spruce up her Scottish fiddling skills. Mostly, she was learning fiddle, though, as she said, "Learning is not the same thing as playing."

Leigh Ann was interested in talking about the history and tra-ditions associated with fiddle, and also interested in the High-land Games themselves, since she came from a Scottish family: the McNaughts.

Leigh Ann and I decided to get lunch together, since she wasn't planning to sit in on the advanced portion of the work-shop. We wandered through the park, weaving through bagpipers and tartan-covered families, off to the concession stands to look for lunch. She'd brought pepperoni rolls in a plastic bag, but I didn't have any food, so I headed for a stand and looked for something appropriately Scottish. Expecting to find haggis or scones, I was surprised to find only typical, all-American fair food: hot dogs, cotton candy, and lemonade. I ended up buying a bowl of potatoes and peppers, thinking them close to Scottish but actually probably more just western Pennsylvanian.

We sat in the shade on a rock wall by her husband, listening to a Scottish rock band and watching a small girl in a white dress do some kind of highland-inspired dance in front of the stage. It was getting hot as the sun climbed in the sky and burned away the mist that had been covering the hills all morning. Leigh Ann passed me a small tube of sunblock, and I thanked her. Judging by her pale skin and freckles, she probably didn't venture anywhere without sunblock. I envied her surety and steadiness: she seemed prepared for every eventuality, with her violin, her pepperoni rolls, her sunblock, her unfailing knowledge of the Highland Games. I couldn't eat more than a few bites of my potatoes and peppers, and I pushed them around in my little Styrofoam bowl, wishing I'd been able to find a little haggis.

As Leigh Ann and I talked, it came out that she'd started playing classical violin, like me, but that her mom had wanted her to play fiddle.

"I guess I've been learning ever since," she said.

I told her that I'd also been inspired by my mom to play fiddle, and she laughed.

"What is it about moms?" she said.

"I know, right?" I said. "I mean, they think they know everything."

We laughed, feeling a sense of connection and camaraderie.

"It's hard to learn alone, though," I admitted. "I've been trying, but it's been something I'm doing pretty much by myself."

"Don't you have any folk jams in your area?" she said.

I shook my head, not really knowing what a folk jam was. "No, I don't think so," I said.

She told me about a folk jam she organized that meets in a park every week in her West Virginia town during the summer, and in a McDonald's during the winter. She said all sorts of people come out for it, with their fiddles, banjos, mandolins, and guitars, and they play mostly old-time music. It sounded wonderful, her folk jam. And the fact that they met at McDonald's seemed funny to me, yet oddly appropriate. McDonald's, after all, *is* a Scottish name.

I chewed on my tasteless potatoes and peppers, thinking, *That's what I need to do, organize a folk jam.* I wanted, suddenly, to do everything Leigh Ann had ever done.

We made our way down to the welcoming ceremonies at noon, where massed bagpipe bands would be playing. There was also the Parade of the Clans, involving one kilted group after another, organized by family names written on banners each group carried as they entered the field and paraded around—Campbells, McArthurs, Stewarts—like a kilted version of a pre-Olympic show. I stood near Leigh Ann, every now and then looking over at her, thinking how Scottish she looked with her pale skin and freckles. Like a real McNaught.

"Are they all really related?" I asked her, waving over at the marching families. She looked at me as if I were a slow child.

"No," she said. "Not really. They join their family groups, and they have to pay a membership fee, just like any other organization."

"Oh," I said, watching as groups of wannabe MacLeods and neo-MacTavishes marched by.

Once all the bands had entered the fields, the clans had marched by, and the Scottish dogs had had their day, the bands gathered midfield and blared out some traditional Scottish tunes, ending with a rousing rendition of "The Bravery of Scotland." By then, I was starting to feel just a wee bit Scottish. Starting to root for this country and its brave-hearted men and women, whatever foes might come their way.

Later that afternoon, Leigh Ann and I took our leave, she to hang out with her husband's family, Clan Campbell, where they'd set up a lunch spread in the picnic area, and I back to the fiddle gazebo to catch the fiddle contest. We promised to write and waved good-bye. Meeting Leigh Ann had felt like good fortune, as if I'd met a fellow traveler on the fiddle path.

The fiddle competition started at I p.m. and went through the afternoon. The contest had specific rules about what the participants would play. In the novice category, competitors had to play an air and then a march, strathspey, or other tune. In the junior and open category, competitors had to play an air, along with a march, strathspey, and reel as a set, meaning the tunes had to blend together with musical transitions in between.

This competition was sponsored by the Scottish Fiddling Revival (SFIRE), a nonprofit organization founded in 1975. The group's mission is to preserve and promote Scottish fiddling, primarily through sanctioning Scottish fiddle contests like this one, certifying judges, and maintaining a list of active fiddle clubs and groups. The Highland Games fiddle contest would be judged by MacKinnon, and not blindly. In this contest, unlike some others, he sat at a table in front of the gazebo where we'd been earlier and watched the participants as they played. Murray had told me it was so the judge could see how the fiddlers moved, since dance-like movements can be as important to Scottish fiddling as the melodies themselves.

First the novice, then the junior, then the open competitors played, each with their required airs and strathspeys and reels. I was waiting especially for Murray and his archrival, a woman who he had told me had won first place over him at the recent Ohio Games in Oberlin: Lydia Byard. She played before Murray, and she reminded me of Charlene Adzima, smiling and moving with the music, tapping her feet. She had a nice tone and good expression.

Then Murray got up and played his tunes: "Bowfiddle Rock," a plaintive, melancholic air he had written himself about a rock in his ancestral Scottish village; "The Murray March"; "Warlock's Strathspey"; and a Cape Breton tune, "Hull's Reel." He played with a forceful motion, as if he pulled these tunes right out of a foggy Scottish history and into Idlewild Park.

As I listened to Murray play, standing up there proudly in his kilt, I marveled at the intensity of this Scottish American subculture that I'd stumbled into. Everyone there thrived on creating a real or imagined Scottish world for themselves and their clans. This culture was a way for them to connect with each other and their heritage, and it didn't seem to make any difference that their version of the heritage might be largely fictional. At this intersection of Scottish and early twenty-first-century western Pennsylvanian cultures, they created for themselves something new, something unique, something vital. It didn't really matter that the whole event might be more Scottish than anything you'd find in Scotland.

It also struck me that Scottish fiddle involves constant improvisation around a theme, and the ability, as MacKinnon had said in the workshop, to always predict what was going to come next and to create a smooth transition into that next tune, using all the snaps and reverse snaps and other tricks one could muster. Though I hadn't been able to get a copy of the music MacKinnon handed out to the participants, I still had the tunes in my head, and I planned to participate in that time-honored fiddle tradition of creating my own settings once I got home.

Knowing it would already be late evening by the time I got back to Ohio, I left before the winners were announced. I'd told my family I'd be back around dinner, and already it would be after eight by the time I made it back to New Concord. Besides, I was tired, and I'd been inundated by Scottish culture. My head hurt, and I was hungry, since I'd only eaten a few bits of the fried potatoes and peppers at lunch. After Murray's performance, I got up from the folding chair and made my way back toward the parking lot, through the ever-present bagpipe music and closed-up rides, trying to find my car in what had turned into a mass of cars since the early morning. I went from one dirt parking lot to another, disoriented and lost, unable to recognize the lot where I'd parked that morning. Finally, I saw the van, got in, and made my way back through the gate and the woods and onto the interstate, this time heading west, toward home. As I drove through the darkening evening, Scottish tunes ringing in my head, I gradually left the highlands of Scotland and returned to the much less fanciful reality of interstate traffic, jostling semitrucks, and western Pennsylvania haze.

A few months later, I e-mailed Murray and asked him who had won and how he had placed.

"Lydia Byard won," he wrote back, simply and dispassionately. "The judge didn't like my tunes, so I didn't place at all."

I wrote back and told him I was sorry, and that I thought he played great.

"Those things happen," he replied. "The judge in Ligonier said the air was totally a wrong piece. Two weeks later, in New Hampshire, I got Best Air award for the competition with the same piece. It's very subjective."

I didn't ask how he felt about the loss, since he seemed to take it in stride. As a good Scottish fiddler, he'd been trained to do just that: transition to the next thing, throw in an ornament or two, improvise a little, and keep on going.

Chapter 9

Deep, Strange Roots
Old-Time Fiddle

When English, Scottish, and Irish immigrants came to America, many of them moved into the Appalachian Mountains. They brought with them old songs and tunes, which in the isolation of the valleys and hollers were preserved and passed down from generation to generation. Fiddlers inherited a wealth of jigs, reels, and strathspeys, and with each generation these tunes merged, mutated, and evolved. And out of that mix developed a distinctively American style referred to broadly as old-time fiddle.

I'd first seen true old-time fiddle playing at the Soakum Festival at the Noble County Fairgrounds near Caldwell, Ohio, before I'd started really getting into fiddling. According to the legend of the festival, Noble County once had along Duck Creek a little town officially called Matrim. Local folk, though, called it Soakum, because of the high liquor prices the townspeople charged their guests. About twenty-five miles from Marietta, Soakum was once a bustling town, serving up "corn squeezin's and applejack" to travelers on their way to and from Marietta, according to the Soakum Festival website. By 1900, however, the town had disappeared.

Every September, the Soakum Festival brings the town and its spirit back to life, with apple butter making, blacksmithing, moonshining, and other old-timey things.

One of the things it doesn't need to resurrect, so much as showcase, however, is old-time fiddling, which still is alive and well in the area. I visited the festival with my friend Robin and our kids, and that afternoon I'd seen some old, bearded guys on a stage, holding their fiddles down low, sawing out tunes that sounded not Scottish, not Irish, but like some American-flavored form that combined elements of both of those.

The violinist in me thought: *Why don't they hold their violins right?* The style among some truly old-time players is to hold the instrument down across the arm, and to play in a quiet, scratchy way that is antithetical to everything you learn when you're taught classical violin. Their strange, droning music entranced me, though. It sounded as old as the hills.

At William's next violin lesson, I'd asked Angela about those fiddlers.

"Yeah, they're something, those old-time guys," she said. "They have a style all their own."

They haunted me, those fiddlers. It was like they had stepped out of history, dusted themselves off, and whipped out the ol' fiddles to play some tunes.

Ken Waldman, a large, bushy-haired, bearded man from Alaska, taught himself old-time fiddle one long, bitter winter, locking himself in his cabin and forcing himself to play. That spring, he emerged from his cabin with a new vocation: fiddling. Now he travels the country, teaching kids and adults about fiddling and poetry.

On one of his visits to New Concord to speak and play at the college, my friend and colleague Jane invited me over to her house to have an impromptu fiddle lesson with Waldman, who is her friend. I was nervous, packing up my violin and heading across the street to where she lives. Jane, her husband Gary, and Waldman greeted me as I stepped inside. I shook his hand, and he smiled back beneath his gray-flecked beard.

"Here for a lesson, I take it?" he said gruffly.

"Yeah, sure," I said. "I'd love one."

"Well, pull out your fiddle, then, and show me what you've got," he said.

Waldman listened to me play "Devil's Dream," the one song I'd memorized from the *Mel Bay* fiddle book. I thought I did pretty good, and I looked at him to see what he thought. Then he said quietly, "Wow, there are a lot of notes there."

I knew he was being critical, but I didn't know what to say.

"It's all in the style," he said, picking up his fiddle and starting to play a tune, quietly, just barely brushing the strings, holding his fiddle down low like I'd seen those fiddlers do at the Soakum Festival.

"This here's a good tune," he said, sawing quietly away on "Old Joe Clark" and asking me to join in. I tried to follow the melody, but not to play loud clear notes. I tried to hold my violin—*fiddle!*—loosely down on my arm.

After a while, he nodded.

"I think you're starting to get it," he said.

∽◯

The earliest recorded fiddle contest in America was held in 1736 in Hannover County, Virginia. Fiddlers came from all around, from cabins in the mountains and towns near and far to compete for the chance to win a violin made in Cremona. Ever since then, contests have been a central part of this country's fiddle culture, bringing together fiddlers and keeping the traditions alive. In the 1920s, Henry Ford, who liked old-time fiddling, hosted fiddle contests at Ford dealerships, drawing crowds who listened to the music and, he hoped, looked at the cars, as well.

Today, there are fiddle contests associated with festivals around the country, with fiddlers often competing for cash prizes and local fame. The largest circuit of fiddle contests feeds into the National Old-Time Fiddlers' Contest in Weiser, Idaho, which began in 1953 and remains America's premier fiddle contest, drawing champions from around the country and the world.

To see what old-time fiddle contests are all about, I took a trip down to Nelsonville, Ohio, to see the annual Old-Time Fiddlers' Championship at Stuart's Opera House. The contest is nationally certified with the Idaho contest, meaning that the Grand Champion of the Ohio event each year is eligible to compete in Weiser. The Nelsonville contest is thus one of the most important in Ohio.

As had become my habit lately with my fiddle journeys, I drove down to Nelsonville alone. Nobody in my family wanted to be dragged several hours south of our house to sit through a fiddle championship.

"Going fiddle hunting again?" my husband asked before I left.

I eyed him skeptically, feeling a bit defensive about my fiddle travels. It was almost like I was having an affair with fiddling. "Yeah, so?"

He shrugged. "Well, have a good time," he said.

I felt that strange combination of guilt and confusion that I'd been feeling lately in regard to my fiddle exploration. But what could I do? I hugged him and said thanks, I would.

"I'll be home around midnight," I said, touching his arm lightly.

"Okay," he said.

"Bye, kids!" I called. Somewhere from the recesses of the house, where they were no doubt ensconced in video game land, I heard them call out faintly, "Bye, Mom!" And I left, happy to be on the next stage of my journey.

It's not easy to get to Nelsonville from New Concord. As the crow flies, it's not so far, but there's no straight shot through the winding, twisting roads and hills of coal country. The most direct way is to head south out of Zanesville on smaller roads through woods, hills, and villages, but it takes about the same time to travel straight down the interstate to Marietta, and then travel back west to Athens and Nelsonville. Because I was traveling alone and wanted to avoid curvy, unpredictable roads and long stretches of uninhabited wilderness, I decided to take the latter route. As I drove, I listened to fiddle tunes piped into the car's stereo from my iPod, as well as the plaintive, punkish tunes of alt-country singers like Gillian Welch and Freakwater. This fiddle and country soundtrack gave me a raw sense of freedom and adventure.

After a couple of hours of driving through the late summer

heat, I arrived in Nelsonville, a small town in southern Ohio, not long before the fiddle championship was to begin. Nelsonville still has the feel of a late–nineteenth century coal boom town, with brick roads and a town square surrounded by buildings in the particular frontier-Victorian style common to Ohio's older, once wealthy towns. Now, though, Nelsonville had the feel of a town just barely holding on. Coal was long gone from this area, and the town was seeking new ways to support itself and its people. On the way into town I'd passed the Rocky Boots Company, one thriving business in the area that has infused the local economy with cash and jobs. And judging from the run-down houses, trailers, and rusty cars I'd passed coming into town, it seemed that Nelsonville could use all the help it could get.

The fiddle championship is part of Nelsonville's Parade of the Hills Festival, an annual community event featuring rides, hot dogs, and cotton candy vendors. On that Saturday afternoon, it looked like all of Nelsonville had turned out for the occasion. The roads leading to downtown were blocked off with police tape and wooden sawhorses, so I had to park on a side street and wade through the families with kids holding cotton candy, past rides and booths and through the small town square, which prominently features Stuart's Opera House.

Built in 1879, Stuart's Opera House was at one time a premier spot for vaudeville, melodrama, and minstrel shows. It was the place where all the coal barons and their families would go for weekend entertainment when the city was booming. By 1924, the boom era of Nelsonville had wound down, and the opera house shut its doors until 1977 when it was bought by a local group and began to host a few shows. In 1980, a fire just about destroyed the building, and in 1997, under new ownership and completely remodeled, the opera house once again opened its doors. Now, with its crisp white walls, gilt windows, rich red curtains, air conditioning, and comfortable seats, it hosts around seventy-five events a year, including the annual fiddle contest. The Old-Time Fiddle Championship has been held for forty years in Nelsonville. It used to be held outside in the public square, but for the past several years it has been inside the opera house.

I entered the opera house through a side door, which led into the basement. Immediately I heard the sounds of fiddlers warming up: those stringy, soulful sounds of practice and hope. Fiddlers from all over the state, as well as several neighboring states, crowded every square foot of this cluttered basement room, sitting on secondhand couches and nestled up against racks of theater clothes. It felt like a locker room before a big game, with everyone working on their chops, psyching themselves up, getting ready for the show.

The first woman I met while wandering through the cacophony of fiddle music and raw, nervous energy was twenty-year-old Krista Solars from Jeromesville, Ohio. In the midst of the noise and precompetition anxiety filling the room, Solars calmly held her violin and sat with her mom, waiting for the championship to begin. Nearby sat Perry McKinley, her neighbor, a guitarist who also makes guitars and fiddles in his spare time. He seemed as proud of Krista as her mom was.

Krista told me she's been playing fiddle on the side for many years. In fact, she had played in this championship for five years, and she placed first in the 18-and-under category back in 2004. Tonight was her big night, and she was hoping to take home a trophy.

"I want to win," said Krista. "I've been wanting to win a long time."

Krista had won a few awards in her performances as fiddler, and she kept coming back for more.

"Her room is full of trophies," her mom, Pam, said.

Krista smiled with a mixture of shyness and pride. "The sun glints off them," she said. "It's really beautiful."

Krista said her music teacher at Oberlin College was Milan Vitek, a violinist from Czechoslovakia who encouraged her fiddling. "He says to me, 'Play some of that folk music,'" she said, laughing. "He really likes it."

She said she was training to be a classical violinist, but liked to keep up with her fiddling, too.

Nearby was ten-year-old Brandon Shull and his father, Greg, who had driven to this contest from their home in Lancaster. Brandon was a quiet boy who had competed in this contest once before, but now he would be competing in the new 12-and-under category. He told me he had plans to play a hoedown called "Liberty" and the "Falling Leaves Waltz." Brandon started playing violin at four and fiddle at eight, and he had recently been taking lessons from Adam Jackson, one of the contest's judges.

"Think that's a conflict of interest?" I asked.

"Nah," his father said. "I hope not."

Brandon told me that he started playing fiddle by ear with a traditional old-time piece called "Soldier's Joy," and that now he "just sort of plays" whatever he feels like playing. His father said that when Brandon was three, the family was at a festival in Baltimore, Ohio, and they saw a family band. Brandon was fascinated by the twelve-year-old playing fiddle, and the next day they called up a local music store and asked about lessons. He's been playing ever since, and has been studying with Jackson for about a year and a half.

Though he supports his son in his musical endeavors, Greg said he isn't a musician himself.

"I don't have much of an ear for music," he said.

∞

There's a lot at stake at these fiddle contests for fiddlers like Krista and Brandon. At the Nelsonville contest, the top fiddler in each category except for the kids would win $300, and the second place winner would get $200. For the kids' category, the top prize was $50, and the second prize was $25. And the winner of the whole thing gets the title "Ohio State Fiddle Champion."

The judges on the night I was there were Bob Acord, Oscar Ball, and Adam Jackson. All the players were thinking of these judges, of their reactions, of how they would respond to their particular tunes.

There were thirty-three contestants in four categories: 12-and-under; 13-to-18; 19-to-54; and 55-and-over. All had signed up on sheets laid out on a large table. I glanced at the names, saw Krista Solars and Brandon Shull, and then I headed up to the backstage area where I thought I might find others waiting for the contest to begin.

Backstage, I found eighty-three-year-old Harold Burns, from Yawkey, West Virginia, sitting alone with his fiddle on a wooden bench. Harold told me he had started playing fiddle when he was forty-five years old, and that in addition to playing fiddle, he made them. He told me he had made thirty-nine fiddles, in fact. He said that he taught himself how to make them from a book, and that he taught himself how to play them by listening to old Clark Kessinger recordings. Things hadn't been going so well for Harold recently, though, since he had a heart attack and a stroke. He said it had been getting harder and harder for him to play fiddle.

"I'm 'bout ready to give it up," he said with a touch of sadness in his voice.

The previous year, he placed third in his age category. This year, he was planning to play "Flowers of Edinburgh" and "Fifty Year Ago Waltz."

"It's fun," he said about the Nelsonville contest. "You meet a lot of friends."

Harold and I chatted for a while, and he said he marveled at the popularity of this contest, at how many people seemed interested in fiddling.

"It's coming back," he said. "Just look at all the young kids. More kids play now. I don't know why."

I sat in a box seat on a plush red chair to the right side of the stage, listening to the first players in the 55-and-over category. One fiddler after another got up in front of the audience and played their hoedowns and waltzes, usually accompanied by guitarists. There was a tense atmosphere, with a lot at stake for these players. I found myself paying particular attention to the fiddlers I'd talked with before the contest. When Harold came on, the fourth to perform in this category, I listened as if he were a long-time friend. He sat on a chair with his cane resting beside him. He had a kind of regal attitude, with his gray beard and blue print shirt, playing a fiddle I knew he had made. He played his "Flowers of Edinburgh" and "Fifty Year Ago Waltz," and I found myself rooting for him.

Next came the 12-and-under category, and the second boy up played fast and furious versions of "Dusty Miller" and "Westphalia

Waltz," wowing the crowd with his black shirt and black cowboy hat. He had the sound and style of a miniature rock star. A few performers later, Brandon Shull took the stage, identified by the announcer only as "Number seven" in his category. With his orange shirt, brown shorts, and the red tape on his fingerboard showing him where to put his fingers, he made his way through "Liberty" and "Falling Leaves Waltz." Following Brandon's performance was a little girl with pigtails, a white shirt, and jeans, playing a tiny violin and tearing through a rowdy rendition of "Bile Them Cabbage Down." In the 19-to-54 category, I recognized Krista playing "Gray Eagle" and "Our Waltz" and wearing her red Western shirt. Maybe it was because I already knew she was a classical violinist, but her playing seemed clean and perfect, at home in a symphony. I found myself wondering: *Would this be authentic enough for the judges?* I knew that one of the criteria they would use was authenticity, but what counts as authentic? Is it possible for fiddling to sound too violin-y? After a while came a blond woman with a purple shirt and jeans playing "Bitter Creek" and "Beautiful Dreamer," wowing the crowd with her style and tone and movements.

Player after player got up in front of that opera house audience and gave the best fiddle performances they could muster. It was dreamlike, really: repetitive and odd, complete with sweaty palms and nervous tics and cheers, with some of the more common fiddle tunes being played several times over the course of the evening. It reminded me of all those orchestra competitions in high school, when our chamber orchestra would travel to Bakersfield or San Diego and all around the state to see who could play the best Bach. Only here, the currency was not Bach but hoedowns.

In the end, after all the players in all the categories had

performed, the judges took a few minutes, scribbling furiously up under their little lights in the balcony, their backs still turned to the stage. The audience stood and milled about, stretching their legs, wandering around in the foyer. I got up and wandered around backstage, where fiddlers joked and laughed, or sat quietly on couches. After ten minutes or so, the audience sat back down and the fiddlers listened intently, and they announced the winners in each category.

Turns out that the charismatic boy who had wooed the crowd with his black cowboy hat and smokin' fiddle playing was named Joe Lautzenheiser, and he walked away with first place in the 12-and-under category. In the 19-to-54 category, the blond woman with the smooth style turned out to be Liz Langford from Tennessee, with Krista coming in second. In the 55 and over category, Harold Burns won second place, after first-place winner Walter Fox.

As he walked out later, Burns slid a $200 check into his pocket and said, smiling at me, "It was worth coming down here."

After this came the championship round, when the winners in each division had to play one more piece, aiming for an extra $300 check, an Ohio State championship plaque, paid entry to the National Oldtime Fiddlers' Contest and Festival in Weiser, Idaho, in June, and recognition in the National Fiddlers' Hall of Fame. Since 1963, the weeklong Idaho festival has been one of the largest gatherings of fiddlers in the country, hosting 350 players from around the world. These fiddlers compete for hundreds of dollars in cash prizes in eight categories, from "small fries" (under 9) to senior-seniors (70 and over). We had another ten-minute break, in which the first-place winners in each category scrambled to get their championship tune ready to play.

I watched as Liz Langford worked on first one tune, then another, with her accompanist.

Then they went out and played, and Liz played in her smooth, slightly Celtic style. No one was surprised when, after the final round, it was announced that she had won the contest. Backstage, I caught up with her. She told me she was twenty-six years old, originally from Dover, Ohio, and living in Nashville. She said she studied classical violin performance at Vanderbilt University, but that she'd started learning fiddle at twelve years old.

"My mom made me," she said, laughing, the backstage lights glinting off her flowing, golden hair.

Chapter 10

Bluegrass Fiddle Boot Camp

That winter, after I'd gone to the Highlands Festival and the fiddle contest, it occurred to me that maybe I could study at home, alone, with books or DVDs. I did some Google searches and landed on a site for Homespun Tapes. In the "About Us" part of the website I found the following philosophy: "Homespun Tapes grew out of the conviction that making music is a positive and beneficial activity, whether you are a professional musician or just learning to play to entertain yourself, your family and friends." I liked the sound of do-it-yourself fiddle instruction.

Happy Traum had published his first instruction manual in 1966 called "Fingerpicking Styles for Guitar," but many students had a hard time learning the music just by reading it from the printed page. So he started producing tapes, at first recording them at home in his living room. He and his wife, Jane, founded Homespun Tapes in 1967, and the company now produces hundreds of DVDs and tapes, available through its website and catalog, to teach people banjo, fiddle, dulcimer, bass, mandolin, piano, and many other instruments and styles.

I looked through the site, entranced. I was especially intrigued by Happy Traum. Was he born with this name—Traum, or, in English, Dream—or had he changed it to this? Either way, I loved it. I ended up ordering a few DVDs on Irish fiddle and old-time fiddle, and a two-DVD set called "Bluegrass Fiddle Boot Camp" featuring "internationally known fiddler and Dobro player" Stacy Phillips. The website said this was a "complete course in which Stacy Phillips unlocks the secrets of playing authentic bluegrass fiddle." I especially liked that "authentic bluegrass fiddle" part. I wanted authenticity, for sure. Plus, I loved the title of the tape. A bluegrass fiddle boot camp seemed to be just what I needed. The DVDs arrived a few days before Christmas, and I put them aside in my closet, feeling a bit guilty that I had ordered them instead of more gifts for the kids.

After Christmas, my husband took the kids to Cleveland to spend a few days at his parents' house, and I stayed home. I'd been looking forward to these few days alone, since I knew that with the family gone, I would finally get to my bluegrass fiddle DVD that I'd been wanting to watch. It was just me, the dogs and the cats, the Christmas tree, and our dead, dark neighborhood in New Concord, with seemingly everyone—students, faculty, and townspeople—off somewhere else.

The fact is, something strange was happening between me and my husband, something I didn't understand. A quiet, unspoken distance had been developing. We were still going through the motions, still eating meals together, still talking about our daily activities, still having something like a normal family life. But something was off. I was so wrapped up in my fiddling and my traveling that I didn't pay it much mind, but by then I'd started to notice. The more I thought about this divide, this distance, this nameless unease, the more I turned to fiddling. It made me happy, gave me hope. I didn't know how to fiddle any more than I knew how to fix my marriage, but by that point learning to fiddle seemed more doable, more possible, more likely. Plus, it reminded me of my mom, made me feel like I was communing with her, doing something she would have liked. I didn't have my mom to talk with about the problems in my marriage, but I had fiddling.

The first afternoon by myself I made green tea with lemon, removed *The Lord of the Rings* from the DVD player, and replaced it with Disc One of *Bluegrass Fiddle Boot Camp*. I settled on the couch with a notebook, my fiddle, and our wirehaired dachshund, Miles. It would be my very own fiddle retreat.

Phillips was wearing a blue button-down shirt with the sleeves rolled up, and he had salt and pepper hair and a scratchy voice. He had a wispy orange feather tied to the scroll of his fiddle, which I thought a nice touch. *I'd like to do something like that with mine, but maybe with a different kind of feather, or something,* I thought.

To play bluegrass, Phillips emphasized in his DVD, a fiddler has to be a good old-time player first, able to play all of the old tunes and styles.

Phillips talked about the importance of having a familiarity with old-time fiddle tunes, like "Blackberry Blossom" and "Soldier's Joy."

"Do learn your old-time fiddle repertoire," he admonished.

After mastering old-time tunes, a fiddler can attempt the faster and louder licks and elaborate solos required by bluegrass.

Well, I've heard *some old-time fiddling,* I thought, remembering those guys at the Soakum Festival. *Perhaps that counts?* This first-things-first approach reminded me of those violin lessons where I had to pass "Lightly Row" before I could progress to "The Merry Farmer" in *Suzuki Book I.* It occurred to me vaguely that I might have been trying to do too much, but the fact is, I had some time on this cold December afternoon, precious time alone with the dog, a magical, post-Christmas quiet settling over the house, and I wanted to learn bluegrass. So I kept watching the DVD.

Phillips talked about how bluegrass music, unlike some other fiddle styles, uses a lot of *legato,* or long, smooth bowings. An exception to the legato tendency, he said, comes with the chops at the beginning of some pieces. Chops are short, sharp notes that introduce the beginning of a solo. I was happy to finally know the origin of the phrase "having chops", since having chops was, after all, one of my goals.

"The first tune we're going to do is not the easiest one," he said in his rough, comforting voice. "In fact, it's one of the hardest in this whole course."

That sounded good to me. I wanted to be an expert, right away, and I thought we might as well start with the hardest tune. He began with the "Why Did You Wander?/Paint the Town/Back to the Old Home" tune family in the key of G, saying that he chose this set of tunes because the solo had been done by so many bluegrass fiddlers: Benny Martin with Flatt & Scruggs, Joe Meadows with Ralph Stanley, various fiddlers with Bill Monroe and the Blue Grass Boys, and Bobby Hicks.

"There's something about this solo that's really important to bluegrass fiddling," said Phillips.

The song began with backup notes to Dave Kiphuth's guitar and vocals: short, syncopated double-stops, with occasional careening slides and fragments of melody between his words, as Kiphuth sang:

> *Why, why did you wander?*
> *Everything's turned upside down . . .*

While Phillips played, the camera zoomed in for close-ups of his fingerboard and his fingers as they moved up and down the ebony. The smooth, simple melody haunted me, and the words were plaintive and meaningful, as if they were a message specifically for me. But watching his fingers move effortlessly through the tune, I wondered if I'd ever feel as free and easy and capable as he did with his fiddle.

After he played through the fiddle riffs and solo of "Why Did You Wander," Phillips analyzed the song. The pattern of the course involved Phillips first playing and then taking apart and explaining the skills, melodies, chords, intervals, and progressions in the tune he just played. He seemed to be an intellectual musician, who apparently valued breaking music into its component parts in order to understand it and then putting it back together. It was more analytical and technical than I expected it to be.

Phillips focused much of his energy on music theory, something I'd never been able to get my head around and was surprised to find in a bluegrass video. Music theory, with its thirds and sevenths and chords and progressions and scales, always struck me the same way math did: boring and incomprehensible. Yet here was Phillips emphasizing the importance of theory to bluegrass music. He talked about the five note and the 3, 4, and 5 chords, and as he did, my mind wandered. I just wanted to learn how to play the music, but here I was getting a theory lesson. Despite myself, though, I put my violin down and began taking notes. If theory was what I needed to learn to play bluegrass, that's what I'd learn.

❧

Bluegrass music began in the 1930s and '40s as a cross between old-time and contemporary pop music, like jazz, blues, and rock. The term itself originated with Bill Monroe's band, the Blue Grass Boys, which was named after Monroe's home state of Kentucky. As the father of bluegrass, Monroe and his band brought together elements of old-time, jazz, folk, and ragtime to create a new, popular form that swept the country. Branching off from Monroe came Earl Scruggs and Lester Flatts, with their band, the Foggy Mountain Boys. And after that came hundreds of other bands that have kept the bluegrass tradition and repertoire alive.

As in jazz music, the instruments in a bluegrass band take turns playing the melody and improvising, whereas in old-time music either all the instruments play together with a single melody, or one instrument is the lead instrument and the others accompany it.

By the late 1950s, the slick Nashville country sound had begun to replace the rougher bluegrass music, and bluegrass slipped into the background as an alternative music now considered roots music. It didn't, however, disappear. Bluegrass festivals and concerts, like Mountain Heir, sprouted across the country. Though it's distinct from popular country music, which went further into the realm of pop music and away from roots music, bluegrass is still going strong.

With the Coen brothers' film, *O Brother, Where Art Thou?* bluegrass music saw a surge of interest, creating a whole new generation of fans. Bands like the Grateful Dead and Bela Fleck brought the sounds of bluegrass into the mainstream, and now Yonder Mountain String Band, Phish, and others are garnering younger fans.

Like many other styles of folk and roots music, bluegrass is a mutating form, always changing, always becoming something new.

Phillips taught several different tunes, including "Why Did You Wander?" "Take This Hammer," "Jimmie Brown, the Newsboy," "Long Journey Home," "All the Good Times Are Past and Gone," and "Salty Dog." I tried to play along with him, following the music in the little booklet that came with the DVDs. I'd stumble around for a while, and then I'd put my violin down and listen to his analysis. Though I grew bored with the music theory, I found myself learning about each of these songs in depth. In the process, I remembered what it's like to learn: starting from scratch, feeling overwhelmed, and learning a bit here and there until it started coming together in my head.

"This course is preparing you for realistic situations," said Phillips.

Often, he said, in a jam session or when playing with a band you haven't played with before, you'll have to play a song in a different key than you're used to. Say you learned a song in G, but the band plays it in A. You need to learn to transpose, to play the same melody and rhythms in a different key. This, said Phillips, was why he was spending so much time on theory and chords.

So I could transpose on the spot if necessary, just by thinking in thirds, fourths, and fifths.

So I could be ready for anything.

The heart of Phillips's lesson, and the thing that has stuck with me longest, was his discussion of *grit*.

"There's been what I would call a regrettable tendency in modern bluegrass fiddlers toward conformity of sound, smoothness, and technical perfection," he said. "Those are certainly worthwhile goals, and I wish I could have them. But we're getting away from the folk roots of bluegrass fiddling."

These roots, he said, emphasized grit, or a rough and ready sound and a bluesy twist, over technical proficiency.

"This is not sloppiness," he said. "But the grit adds something to the energy of the playing. Technical perfection is not the be all and end all of bluegrass and folk fiddling in general."

As he talked, I was thinking: *He's right.* What I need to learn is grit. I need to have grit. I am too smooth, too perfect, too obsessed with technical perfection. With a perfect marriage, a perfect life.

In fiddling and life, I need to get me some grit.

Grit seemed to be why I was attracted to fiddling in the first place. As a classical player, I was trained to play pure, smooth notes. Just as I was trained to be a good girl. But now, in midlife, I needed some dirtiness, rawness, and roughness. Something that would see me through whatever was hurtling my way.

Smoothness, purity, and good-girliness, after all, can get you only so far. Those only worked if things went as planned, if marriages stayed happy, if life stayed predictable. They didn't work so well when things started to fray.

Then he laughed and said, "That's my excuse for playing out of tune."

Which, come to think of it, was another reason I needed grit: to cover over the raw places, the things I didn't know how to do, the things I still needed to learn. Grit makes everything sound better, even if you're actually faking it.

"You want to be able at least to play something that resembles the melody of the tune," he said. He emphasized that a fiddler needs to listen to the melodic contour and the rhythm, and to try to mimic these. He taught some basic riffs and bowings, including the Georgia Shuffle and the Nashville Shuffle, which involve different pairings of notes slurred together or played separately. These riffs, he said, are useful as a basic repertoire of skills, and they can be pulled out in many different songs and different situations.

"Those kind of licks are really handy when you don't know your way around a tune," Phillips said.

There's an art to faking it. Faking it crosses improvisation with self-assured theatrics. In faking it, you don't know exactly where you're going, but you have enough skill to make it sound good, anyway. And no one ever knows the difference.

For so long in my life, I'd been assuming that if I just played by the rules, and did the same things over and over, playing by the music, I'd do fine. But I was learning that when events happen that you don't expect, playing by the rules doesn't work very well. Unpredictable things sometimes happen, people grow distant, problems arise, and these events require one to improvise. And perhaps this is what my mom wanted me to learn all along: not particular fiddle tunes, but the *spirit* of fiddling. The ability to improvise, change, and evolve. I needed to learn to take what was given to me and try new things, new melodies, new riffs. And if I played something strange or out of tune or not quite right, that would be fine. That's what faking it is all about: being able to make it sound like it's all part of the music you wanted to create in the first place.

"People might actually be fooled into thinking you wanted to play that," Phillips said. "Don't let them know that you're faking it."

Chapter 11

Klezmer in Cleveland

While searching YouTube for clips of fiddle playing, I ran across a short video of Itzhak Perlman with a group of folk musicians, playing a strange, rapid, cascading music unlike any I had ever heard. Joining several other musicians and clearly improvising, he smiled, laughed, rocked, swayed, and threw himself into a haunting interpretation of a folk melody. I loved Perlman's classical violin playing, but I'd never seen him look so free, so happy, so *folksy*. I was entranced. This music spoke to me in a deep, inexplicable way, as if I'd heard it before. Looking at the description of the clip, I saw it was called klezmer music, but I'd never heard that term before. I knew I needed to find out more.

So I got several books from the library, and looked around online, and I quickly learned that klezmer music has been a part of Jewish culture for centuries. "Klezmer" means "village musician" in Yiddish, and it refers to a folk tradition of wandering musicians, called klezmorim, who play for Jewish holidays and weddings. Early klezmer instruments included various kinds of strings, drums and horns, and in the past couple of centuries it had evolved into a form using fiddle, clarinet, guitar, drums, and other instruments.

Henry Sapoznik, in his *Klezmer! Jewish Music from Old World to Our World,* argues that "The Klezmer's story . . . is Jewish history in miniature, a distilled panorama of growth and preservation, of triumph over adversity, and of unimagined revitalization and renewal." And the more I thought about klezmer music, the more I realized it spoke to me, perhaps in deeper ways than any other form of fiddling. My father was a Holocaust survivor, who had barely survived the war with his family in Budapest. I'd grown up with stories of his trauma, starvation, and fear. But I'd also grown up with stories of how my grandfather was a concert pian-ist before the war, and how my grandmother liked to sing opera music. I'd always liked imagining that pre—war time of music and beauty, and I had since I was a child fantasized about being a gypsy violinist wandering through the Hungarian countryside with bells on my ankles, playing around campfires.

Learning that there was such a thing as klezmer music, a whole Jewish folk tradition of fiddling that had survived centu-ries, intrigued me and gave me hope.

The fact is, I was, that spring, in need of hope. In January, my husband had announced that he wanted an in-house separation. I'd thought something like this might happen, but the reality of it still came as a surprise. I was sad and confused by his request to separate, and even more so because he wanted the separation to be *in our house.* That young, blond-haired, bad/good boy I had married impulsively so many years before, raised two children, and built a life with had become a deeply unhappy, uncommuni-cative middle-aged man. I didn't understand why, and he didn't tell me. I was hurt and bewildered, but he was adamant. He said he would sleep in his basement office and we'd see each other at meals. He blew up a brown, velour air mattress that we'd bought a couple of years before for a camping trip, and I brought him some sheets. I shook them out, spread them over the mattress, tucked in the corners, and folded a blanket on top. I sat there on the sinking edge of the mattress for a moment, looking at it and feeling like a mom helping her teenage son set up his new place.

"Thanks," he said.

"Sure," I said, holding back tears. "I guess this'll be comfortable for you."

"It's just an experiment," he said. "To see if we can be civil to each other."

I looked at him blankly. I couldn't comprehend what he meant. It seemed we were plenty civil to each other; it was closeness we were missing. It didn't make sense that more remoteness would bridge the growing distance between us.

"I just really don't understand," I said weakly.

He shrugged and then smiled a half smile that turned into a vague grimace. His expressions were confusing, strange, inscrutable. I didn't know how to interpret them. Looking at him, I realized that though I still loved this man I had spent my whole adult life with, I really didn't know who he was, or what he wanted, or what would make him happy.

At night, I'd lie upstairs on our queen-size bed, listening to distant trains and dogs, thinking of him down there—directly below me—also distant, in his own world. The fact that he slept on our camping mattress seemed especially ironic. We were supposed to use it for fun family vacations, not for an in-house separation.

So this was our life for several months, living together but separated. Talking but not talking. Together but apart. It was like a melody I had never heard before, a tune that made no sense. I listened closely, trying to play along with it, but it was in some strange, difficult key, and I couldn't quite get the notes right.

In the midst of this shaky, uncertain period at home, klezmer music seemed all the more appealing. It might have been an escape, or a survival strategy, or both, but I was clinging to fiddle music more than I ever had. This was my realm, something I understood, territory I could explore. And it seemed to have lessons for me that might help me to survive whatever happened with my marriage.

Late one night while my husband slept downstairs, I searched out klezmer bands on the Web and found Yiddishe Cup, a band that had formed in 1988. Yiddishe Cup's website explained that "klezmer music is a hybrid of Eastern European Jewish folk music, American swing, Yiddish theater tunes, and Israeli horas." Looking at the site's calendar, I saw the band would be playing for the Purim celebration in April at the Park Synagogue in Cleveland Heights. I knew I needed to attend this performance.

The next day I called my mother-in-law Sherry, who lives in Cleveland, and told her that I'd be coming up to see the band Yiddishe Cup performing at the Park Synagogue. Without hesitation, she said she'd meet me there. She sounded afraid for me, hearing that I'd be going to a synagogue by myself. We talked about how we might be able to go to a deli or something for dinner. I envisioned that part of Cleveland Heights to be some kind of Brooklyn-like Jewish neighborhood with a deli on every corner.

I met her in the synagogue's parking lot. She got in my van, and we proceeded to a BP station for sas before driving around to find someplace to eat. Sherry had grown up in a Slovenian Catholic family nearby, and she remembered this area from high school as a lively hub. Now, though, it had become a dead zone, with a few video rental stores and hair salons anchored by a Walmart and a Home Depot. In a parking lot behind the mostly defunct mall, we found the only restaurant in the immediate vicinity: an International House of Pancakes. We looked at each other and shrugged. It was no Jewish deli, but it looked like the best we could do.

Inside, she ordered blueberry pancakes, and I looked half-heartedly for matzah ball soup on the menu. Finding none, I settled for a veggie omelet. While we waited, drinking our iced tea, I tentatively approached the subject of what had been happening between me and her son.

"I guess I have something to tell you," I said, twirling my straw in the glass.

She looked at me, surprised, concerned. "What's wrong?" she said.

"We're having problems," I said. "In our marriage. We're having problems."

Sherry's pretty face suddenly appeared drawn and worried. Sherry had always been so loving to me, so kind, and I was sorry to have to tell her something like this.

The waitress brought our food, breakfast for dinner, and placed it nonchalantly on the table. "You ladies want anything else?" she asked in a distinctively Cleveland drawl.

"No, we're fine, thanks," said Sherry.

She smiled a little at the waitress and then turned to me, a look of concern in her eyes. "Really?" she asked. "Are you okay? What's going on?"

I shrugged. "I dunno," I said, picking at my omelet. "He

says he's not happy. We're separated now, in the house, and he's thinking of moving out."

Sherry looked shocked, a hint of tears rising in her pretty blue eyes, and I felt like I needed to apologize for something. She held her hand out across the table and squeezed my arm.

"I'm so sorry," she said. "I never thought this would happen to you two. You always seemed so, well, so meant for each other."

I tried to smile, even as I was fighting back tears. I really didn't want to cry in an IHOP, before a Purim celebration, in front of my mother-in-law. Maybe she was right. Maybe we had been meant for each other, at one time. We'd married so quickly, so impulsively, but we had stayed together for eighteen years. We'd been friends, companions. We had the kids. I thought we would be staying together for the rest of our lives. *That* was the melody I had been expecting, the one I'd been playing. But had we been meant for each other? I didn't know. I didn't know what I thought about anything anymore.

"Yeah," I said. "I don't know. I really don't know what's going to happen."

"Well, whatever happens, know that we're here for you," Sherry said, squeezing my arm again. "Okay?"

"Okay," I said, feeling sorry for myself, ashamed, and grateful, all at once. Sherry was so loving, so kind. I could lose my husband, I thought, but I never wanted to lose her.

"I love you," she said.

"I love you, too," I said, my voice catching in my throat.

"Ready to go see what's going on at the synagogue?" she asked, smiling brightly.

"Sure," I said. "Let's go."

We had a hard time finding the synagogue again, since it had only a small driveway, and a thick swathe of trees blocked the view from the road. But once we got in there, we saw it was a large complex, with outbuildings that looked like classrooms and a large sanctuary hall. People were piling in. The men wore yarmulkes, and the children all wore costumes: Sponge-Bob SquarePants, Superman, princesses. I thought this strange. Wouldn't they be dressed as Jewish figures, or something? This just seemed like a version of Halloween.

I had read a little about Purim on Wikipedia before I'd left home. Something about Esther helping to save the Jews from Haman. I knew costumes were involved, but I wasn't sure how much the adults participated. I'd brought a purple velvet hat, just in case, but Sherry said that since none of the adults we saw in the parking lot had costumes on, I could probably leave it in the car. As we went into the sanctuary, a slow-moving police car prowled the lot like a shark, apparently there for Purim crowd control. But the crowd didn't seem to need to be controlled; the little SpongeBobs and fairy princesses were excited, but they dutifully followed their parents into the sanctuary.

Inside, a man at the door handed us little metal noisemakers that buzzed when you whirled them around, and we found some seats among a cacophonous crowd of little Supermen, proud grandparents, and frazzled parents chasing after toddler princesses. At the front, a man dressed in a blond wig and a dress led the Megillah reading. All around us, there was a buzzing sound from noisemakers that people whirled around every time Haman's name was mentioned in the reading. And, then, whenever Mordecai's name was mentioned, the crowd cheered. Soon, I got the hang of it. Haman: noisemaker. Mordecai: cheer. As in, *Now there was in the royal palace at Shushan a certain Jew named Mordecai* [CHEER] . . .

Now, King Ahasuerus promoted Haman [NOISEMAKERS], *the Agagite, and gave him a place above all the princes who were with him.* And on a child's level, I could understand why this teaching works.

I got it. Mordecai: good guy. Haman: bad.

I was getting anxious to see the band, though. I thought it might play as part of the reading, but after a while I realized that we'd have to go find it. So we threaded our way out of the sanctuary, into the fellowship hall, and there they were: the members of Yiddishe Cup, warming up on their fiddle and clarinet and drums, in all their Hawaiian-shirted glory.

As the band warmed up, I talked for a few minutes at the stage with Steve Ostrow, the band's fiddler. He was a crazy combination of cultures and styles, a true amalgamation. He wore a hula skirt made of strips of green and yellow plastic over his pants, a gray sweatshirt, and a vest embroidered with shiny thread and beads that looked slightly, but not totally convincingly, old-world. He also had a wig made of green foil strips, and on top of that a straw hat. This was part of Yiddishe Cup's *shtick*: to combine musical and cultural elements humorously, irreverently. They were all about the party.

In fact, it wasn't just Yiddishe Cup's philosophy: it was the philosophy of klezmer music itself. Klezmer is a combination of styles, picking up whatever lies in its path. Beginning with Eastern European folk songs, and once in America gathering in elements of swing, jazz, country, and rock, it is a genre constantly in flux, constantly evolving, and always having fun. In this way, Steve and his crazy clothes perfectly expressed the spirit of klezmer music.

Steve told me he'd been trained as a classical violinist. He'd studied at Eastman School of Music, specializing in classical guitar. At twenty-seven, he switched to violin, and he earned his master's degree in violin from the University of Akron in 1990. He played full-time in the Akron Symphony and did these other gigs in his spare time. He'd been with Yiddishe Cup since 1993. He wasn't Jewish, though, and he didn't really even think of himself as a klezmer musician, exactly, since he was a musician first, but that he played lots of different styles. In fact, he said the next day he would be playing at an Easter service, and the night before he'd been at a bar in downtown Cleveland playing with a country band.

"So how would you describe Yiddishe Cup's approach to klezmer?" I asked him.

"It's not authentic, but klezmer music isn't authentic," he said. "It's always changed and evolved. It's not one thing, you know. It's all music. Folk songs, Bruce Springsteen, everything. It's all music to me."

And once they started playing, I heard what he meant: Yiddishe Cup played a strange, rowdy mixture of swing, Eastern European tunes, Israeli folk tunes, along with klezmerized versions of Jimmy Buffett and Bruce Springsteen hits. And when they played "Camptown Ladies" and "Rawhide," accompanied by the squeal of the clarinet and the klezmer sound of the fiddle, it made perfect sense.

"This is a Mitzvah band," Ostrow told me. "A party band. We have fun. That is what music is all about."

There isn't one kind of klezmer music; it just keeps changing, adapting, gathering in itself whatever crosses its path.

It's not authentic, but klezmer music isn't authentic.

৩৶

Munching on the *hamantashen* and dancing, the kids and adults followed the band's music, circling in and out in ever more complicated patterns. Throughout it all, an energetic man in a button-down pink oxford shirt led people through the dances, getting them excited, showing them the moves. At first I didn't know who he was.

"Do you think that's the rabbi?" I whispered to Sherry, feeling ashamed that I wouldn't know this, being half Jewish and all.

She shrugged. "Would a rabbi be dancing like that?"

"I don't know," I said. "Would he?"

I took notes and pictures, wanting to record the organized chaos swirling around me. It was only my second time in a synagogue, despite my Jewish roots. The first time I'd been in a synagogue had been the summer before in Budapest, when I visited the Dohány Synagogue, following the trail of the Holocaust that my father's family had followed. But that was more like a museum, a place marking the past. This was a lively, living place, hosting a real festival. A "Jewish Mardi Gras," the band leader, Bert Stratton, had called it.

Gradually, the dancers and kids and families thinned out, grabbing their last bit of *hamantashen* and retrieving their coats. Then, to my dismay, Bert pointed me out to the crowd.

"Tonight we have with us Vivian Wagner, who came all the way from New Concord to hear us play." I smiled and waved, self-conscious and suddenly shy. "And now, Mrs. Greenman has in-sisted that we play a polka for our last song, and that's what we're going to do."

They started in on the polka, and Sherry looked surprised. "I didn't know they did polkas in synagogues," she said.

She knew her polkas, but the Slovenian kind.

"It's a little different from a Slovenian polka," she said, but she was smiling anyway.

Then, suddenly, catching me unawares, the pink-shirted man rushed over and grabbed my hand, pulling me into the manic, musical fray.

"Let's polka," he said, and it was more a command than a request.

"I'm Dan," he said breathlessly. "The band's *schtickmeister*. I keep things moving, keep people dancing, keep things lively."

Ah, I thought, so *that's* what he is. A *schtickmeister*.

Dan twirled me around and around the dance floor, while I held my pen and notebook at his back, clung to his pink shirt, and tried to keep up with his dance steps. Once in a while, I'd see Sherry's blurred face going by, and she'd smile and wave. I could hear her thinking: *This is why I needed to come here with her. To protect her from men like that. Crazy polka-dancing, pink-shirted men.*

After it was over, Sherry and I walked to the car, making our way in the dark through the throngs of tired, spent Purim revelers.

At my van, she gave me a hug.

"Please know you can talk to me whenever you need to," she said. "And whatever happens, you'll always be our daughter."

I stayed in her hug, feeling her warmth, unable for a moment to let go. And then I did. I got back in the van, and I drove toward home, the manic, authentic, inauthentic sounds of klezmer music racing through my head, buoying me forward along the interstate.

Chapter 12

Swinging Through the Southwest

In May, my husband moved out of our house and into a little apartment by the railroad tracks on the other side of the village. After he left, I crumpled onto the kitchen floor and cried. Cried for everything I didn't understand. Cried for him, for me, for the kids. Miles came over to where I sat, slumped and defeated, gently touching his cold, wet nose to my arm.

Numb and trying to deal with the shock of my husband's leaving, I planned a trip. But this time, I'd take the kids. Just the kids and me, on a trip. Kind of fiddle-related, kind of family-related, but mostly a chance to get the hell out of town and try to collect my thoughts, my feelings, myself.

A flight response.

I went on Orbitz to make reservations for a ten-day trip through the Southwest. We would fly into Las Vegas, rent a car, visit my great aunt Edith and her daughter Marlene in Henderson for a few days, and then we'd start heading east through the desert. I figured we could stop at the Grand Canyon; head down to Lakewood, New Mexico, to visit my aunt Lucy, who lives in an

RV; and then, finally, go over to Snyder, Texas, to the West Texas Western Swing Festival, where I knew I'd find some fiddlers. It was an impulsive trip, an expensive trip, and a barely planned trip, but a trip that I felt I needed. These were relatives on my mom's side: strong women, all of them. And right then, I needed to remember that I'd come from a long line of women, from the pioneers who crossed the country in covered wagons, raised cattle, and settled ranches, to Aunt Edith, who had made it to ninety-two and still walked a mile a day. I needed to be with my women.

At the airport in Las Vegas, we got our car, a white Nissan Rogue. The kids were impressed, and I was excited to try out a new car. Gas pushed $4 a gallon that summer, which made driving a crossover SUV that got only marginal gas mileage not the smartest thing to do. But this was an adventure, and that Nissan Rogue made me happy. We drove into Henderson, a suburb of Las Vegas still riding the housing boom that would soon crash, to the gated community where Marlene, her husband Jerry, and Edith lived.

When we got to their beautiful house, on a dry ridge overlooking the Las Vegas strip miles away, I hugged Marlene and Edith. The kids ran to put their swimsuits on so they could swim in the black marble pool out back.

"How have you been?" Marlene asked as we stood in the kitchen.

"Oh, okay," I said, realizing that I wasn't going to tell her anything about what was happening right then. It was too new, too fresh, and I didn't know how to describe it. I wasn't sure how it would all end. "Just kind of tired."

"Yeah," she said. "Well, stay a few days, and relax, okay?"

I nodded. "Thanks, Marlene," I said, feeling suddenly safe.

Edith touched my arm with her gnarled, wrinkled hand, and I turned toward her and hugged her thin body to mine. "It's good to see you," she said softly in her shaky voice, up by my ear. "Good to have you here."

"Thanks, Aunt Edith," I said, trying not to cry. "I'm happy to be here."

We stayed a few days. Every morning I'd leave the kids with Marlene and walk out on the sidewalks, criss-crossing the dry ridges through the wealthy housing development. On these walks, I'd call my husband and ask him various themes on the same question. *Why?* Why, why, why? Would he reconsider? What was going to happen? What was he thinking? What were we going to do?

There was an adamancy to his voice, though, that scared me. He was not going to move back. It was over. He made that quite clear. Devastatingly clear. On one of these mornings, after a particularly long, confusing phone call with him, I found myself sitting in the dirt by the golf course, bawling in the hot, late-morning sun, as if I had swerved off the road and crashed into the railing. A real wreck.

After a few days in Henderson, I knew it was time to leave. The kids and I said good-bye to Marlene and Edith, promising to write, to keep in touch.

"You take care, okay?" Marlene said, eyeing me. I wondered if she could sense that something was wrong, that I wasn't telling her everything.

"I will, Marlene," I said. "Thanks. Thanks for everything."

We got into the Rogue, waving at Marlene and Edith, who stood bent over in the driveway, smiling, blowing us a kiss.

We made our way out through the gate and onto the highway, and we drove most of the day through the hot, dry desert, over Hoover Dam, toward the Grand Canyon. Rose sat in the back, watching DVDs on a portable DVD player, and William sat in front, with a map, helping me navigate the freeways. At the Grand Canyon, we went to the visitor's center, where we had a picnic lunch and saw an IMAX movie about the first rough, dangerous rafting trip taken through the canyon on the Colorado River by John Wesley Powell and his men in 1869.

Leaving the visitor's center, we drove over to the canyon's rim, battled traffic, and finally found a place to park. We stood at the edge of the canyon, looking over the guardrail, watching a family of Japanese tourists take pictures of themselves with its red and brown expanse as a backdrop.

"Well, what do you think, kids?" I asked them.

"I thought it would be bigger," William said.

"Bigger?" I asked, feeling suddenly defensive for the Grand Canyon. "It's the biggest damned canyon in the world."

He shrugged, looking unimpressed.

"I think it's nice," Rose said.

The three of us were hot and tired from the hours of traveling, though, and I had to admit: William was right. From up there, by the guardrail, after a long, hot day of desert driving, that canyon could have been bigger.

"Well, let's keep driving along the rim, and maybe it'll be more interesting down the road."

"Can we go white-water rafting?" Rose asked. "That looked like fun."

I nodded, thinking that *would* be fun. "Yeah, it did, didn't it?" I said. "Let's plan on it sometime soon. We can't go on this trip, but we can plan another to do that."

"Great!" she said. "I can't wait."

And right then, a thought occurred to me: we had more freedom now, me and the kids. If we wanted to go white-water rafting, we could just plan it. Not that we couldn't have gone before, but it seemed more complicated then. Now, well, we could do whatever the hell we wanted.

I drove along the rim, stopping at another spot where we could see more colors in the canyon walls.

"A little better from here, isn't it?" I asked William.

"Yeah," he agreed. "It's better perspective from here." He took out his Flip camera and made a short video of the canyon, with Rose and me standing on the edge. Rose held her hands in front of her face, like a movie star avoiding the paparazzi. Then we piled back into our Rogue and drove through the desert, past a Navajo reservation, with its trailers and dogs tied out in the sagebrush.

"This is a reservation we're going through, kids," I said.

"It *is*?" Rose asked. "Are you *sure*? It doesn't *look* like a reservation."

"Well, it is," I said. "Navajos live out here, in these trailers. Indians don't all live in teepees, you know."

Rose didn't look like she believed me, quite, but I didn't know how else to convince her.

We worked our way down to Flagstaff, where we stayed at a Hilton Garden Inn nestled up along the city's pine-covered volcanic hillside. The next morning, we traveled on to Albuquerque, stopping for lunch at a dusty, forlorn Mexican restaurant in Gallop, where we had enchiladas and tortilla chips. In the next booth, an Indian family ate their meal and eyed us sideways now and then, while an air conditioner whirred in the window. In Albuquerque, we stayed at a Hampton Inn, swimming for a while in the leaf and dust-covered pool in a hot, dry breeze. We kept moving, moving, moving.

The next morning, we proceeded to southeastern New Mexico, stopping for a while in Roswell to go to the International UFO Museum and Research Center. The story of aliens that had supposedly crashed outside Roswell back in the 1940s fascinated the kids. We made our way through the museum, listening for a while to a tour guide who explained why the theory that the alien craft had actually been a weather balloon was not in line with the facts.

"Was it really an alien ship?" Rose whispered to me as we listened to the guide.

"I don't think so," I said. "But let's look around and see what you think."

Both kids studied the photographs and newspaper accounts carefully, their eyes wide with a mixture of interest, skepticism, and amazement that there would be a museum devoted to something even their mom doubted was true.

"I don't think it was really an alien ship," Rose whispered to me. "It looks more like it was just tinfoil."

I nodded. "Yeah, you're probably right," I said.

Outside, I took pictures of the kids by the alien-shaped street lamps, and we looked in the storefronts selling alien balloons, alien glasses, alien T-shirts, and alien postcards. Then we headed down to Carlsbad, where we checked in to a Holiday Inn. The kids swam in the pool for a while—consolation for the long drive—before we made our way out to see Aunt Lucy, my mom's sister. She had divorced years before and remarried a man named Dick; they'd lived here in an RV park for a few years. Her RV park, off the highway about a mile and out in the middle of the flat, New Mexican desert, was called SKP Escapees. SKP, she had told me over the phone, stands for "Special Kind of Person," the name of their RVers group.

"Hey, look who's here," Lucy called out as we pulled into the small driveway by her RV. Lucy was stocky and strong, outspoken and forceful. She hugged me and the kids, holding us tightly. The last time I'd seen her had been at my mom's funeral a few years before, and it was good to be with her again. "Look how you've grown," she said to them.

Dick smiled and shook my hand. "Nice to see you again," he said.

We went inside their fifth-wheel trailer, which was semi-permanently parked in the space. They lived there with a little overweight dachshund, and we sat in the small living room with square windows looking out at the flat desert all around, visiting and catching up.

"So this is the life out here," I said. "I could see myself getting used to this."

I'd avoided telling Lucy what was happening in my life, since I wasn't sure myself, exactly. I didn't want to have to explain. So I kept mute, and played along like all was fine.

"We have a lot of freedom," Lucy said. "We come and go as we please, and take trips when we can afford it. We've gotten to know all the neighbors, and this is home."

As we talked, the kids petting and playing with their dog, I began to feel some strength returning to me. Even though I didn't tell her what was happening with me, I found it comforting being with her nonetheless. With her husky voice, short hair, and guttural laugh, she talked about their life in the desert, and I thought of all these women in my family who had had rough times and survived. From my grandmother, who ran away from a poor home in the Colorado Rockies and made a life for herself, to my mom, who beat all odds and became a mathematician, to her sister, Lucy, here before me, divorced, remarried, and now with a new life here in the desert. And I began to catch a glimpse of many possible futures for myself, including a brief fantasy of living in an RV in the middle of the New Mexican desert. It felt liberating, freeing, exhilarating. I began to think: *Maybe I'll be able to survive this divorce after all. Maybe I'll live through this, and be able to be strong, and be a good mom for the kids, and do what I want and need to do without a husband. Why not? Survival is in my blood.*

We went to lunch at a Chinese restaurant in Artesia, and afterward we walked around for a while in the white hot sun, looking at bronzed statues of early settlers, ranchers, and cowhands in the area. As the sun got lower in the sky, we bid farewell to Lucy and Dick.

"Keep sending me your e-mails," I told Lucy.

She hugged me and the kids. "You keep in touch," she said, and I told her I would. Then the kids and I got back in our Rogue, which we'd parked strategically in the shade of a eucalyptus tree, and drove back to our hotel down in Carlsbad.

Feeling stronger, more capable, and more myself, I headed east in the morning with the kids on Route 180 toward Snyder, Texas. It was windy and hot, and I drove past mesquite and creosote bushes, alfalfa farms, and oil wells bobbing like strange, mechanical dinosaurs, their steel feet curling around and around as they pushed their pumps deep into the ground, brought up thick, rich oil, and pushed their pumps in again. That morning, crossing the bleak landscape bordering New Mexico and Texas, I felt better than I had in months.

The air smelled like oil, and we passed a few refineries, with their long, white, complicated pipes snaking in and out of themselves. We moved ahead an hour into Central Time when we crossed the border into Texas. The landscape around us was dry and dusty, with occasional hills and willow-filled washes. William sat in the front seat following our progress on the AAA map of the Southwestern states, and Rose sat in the back watching a Harry Potter DVD.

Snyder lies on the west Texas plains, about eighty miles south of Lubbock. Snyder's history began in 1878, when William Henry Snyder, a buffalo hunter and trader, built a trading post on the banks of Deep Creek. A town made up of buffalo hide tents, it acquired the name "Hide Town." By 1882, it had a town plan and a school, and in 1884 it became the county seat of Scurry County.

In 1948, oil was discovered north of town, and Snyder became an oil boomtown. Its prosperity lasted only until 1951, however, when the boom tapered off along with the oil. Since then, it's been struggling to bring itself back and making some modest progress. The town has a community college, Western Texas College, and an art museum with eighty bronze statues and two hundred paintings. Mostly it has a few gas stations, a courthouse, some motels, and some boarded-up mystery buildings. That's about it. A billboard along a nearby road advertising the town has an oil well with sparkly oil pouring from the top, but that seemed overly optimistic for current-day Snyder.

The small west Texas town does have one thing to brag about, though: the annual West Texas Western Swing Festival, which occurs every June at the Scurry County Coliseum. The Coliseum is a grand name for a large, brown, square building on the west edge of town. As we pulled into the Coliseum's parking lot, we saw the sign: WELCOME, WEST TEXAS WESTERN SWING FESTIVAL, JUNE 11–14. RVs and campers, housing all the on-the-road retirees coming to the festival, filled the parking lot. Golf carts for shuttling people back and forth from their RVs stood lined up at the door.

"Ready for the western swing festival?" I asked the kids as we got out of the car, a dry wave of oppressive heat hitting us as soon as we opened the doors.

William rolled his eyes. "How long is it going to be?" he asked.

"Yeah," Rose added. "How long do we have to stay here?"

"Just a few hours," I said. "I just want to hear a few of the bands."

The kids followed me through the dusty parking lot to the main door, dragging their feet. They didn't mind a road trip across several states, but a western swing festival was too much.

At the door, a man in a plaid shirt and cowboy hat swung the door open for me.

"There you go," he said in a dry Texas drawl, half bowing to the three of us. "Enjoy the show."

I paid my $20 admission, happy to find that kids under twelve were free. As we walked in and saw a sea of gray hair and cowboy hats, I realized mine were about the only kids there, anyway. I got a program for the festival, along with a yellow badge that read I WENT FIDDLIN' AROUND IN SNYDER TEXAS.

The Coliseum had a cement floor and bleachers lining the walls. A dance floor with red, white, and blue fringe and decorated with flags in the corners had been set up. Here, cowboy-hatted men and sequined, gray-haired partners did two-steps and waltzes in time to the music. The stage stood at the far end of the expansive, high-ceilinged building, with folding chairs lined up so people could sit and listen. And the sweet, piercing sound of western swing music filled the hall.

The kids and I settled into three empty seats and began listening to the River Road Boys, with fiddler Clyde Brewer. They were all dressed up in matching white shirts with red stripes of southwest design and large off-white cowboy hats. Behind the stage hung a large American flag, along with a wooden cutout of Texas painted red, white, and blue and fringed in white lights. The River Road Boys had a big band feel, and they played "Bandera Waltz," "Basin Street Blues," "My Window Faces the South," and many other songs. As the band played, the people danced.

While the music continued, I left the kids in their seats for a minute and walked over to the table stacked with the band's CDs. Behind the table stood Vivian Hauser and Sedonia Brewer, wives of men in the band. I asked Sedonia, a regal woman with white hair and a true western name, if she ever danced.

"Not usually," she said. "Out of respect for the guys."

Sometimes, though, she admitted, she'd dance with a group of friends. She and Vivian talked excitedly about the western swing cruises they'd gone on, and they said they *did* dance on those. I bought an instrumental twin fiddle CD featuring Clyde and another fiddler, and then I went back to where the kids sat, fidgeting and eyeing me with looks that said they wanted to go. *Now.* I smiled.

"Just a little longer," I said.

After a while, a young boy came onstage: the band introduced him as six-year-old Colby Sheppard. Dressed as a cowboy, complete with a large white hat, he sang "Home in San Anton," and then he brought out his fiddle to play a tune William and

I recognized: "Bile Them Cabbage Down." When he finished, Clyde handed the violin back to his mom offstage, saying: "Here, Mama, take this Stradivarius and put it somewhere safe." The crowd broke out in laughter. Then Colby sang "Bob Wills Is Still the King," with inflections and a sense of personality way beyond his age. "You just can't live in Texas unless you've got a lot of soul," he sang, emphasizing the word "soul." Later, his mom told me he'd been playing violin less than a year and singing since he was three. I picked up his business card, asking him if he wanted to keep doing music.

"You betcha," he said with all the assurance of a six-year-old Texan.

After Colby's performance, the band played "Route 66," tracing some of the places the kids and I had just come through: Gallop, Flagstaff, Kingman. I looked over at the kids and smiled, but they didn't look amused. I knew they couldn't wait to be away from this western swing music. They were bored. They were frustrated. They had had enough of Mom's festival.

I couldn't help but think, though, that at that point they were partly just playing the *role* of bored kids. I knew in some ways they were enjoying this trip, this crazy adventure.

At the snack bar, I bought Rose Reese's peanut butter cups and William a Three Musketeers bar. A few minutes later they said they were still hungry, so we went back to get Rose nachos and William popcorn. On one of these trips back and forth, a large cowboy with a blue plaid shirt and a ten-gallon hat ran into Rose, almost knocking her over. "Oh, I'm sorry, little lady," he said, looking at her with a mixture of surprise and slight irritation. Clearly, people shorter than four feet had to watch their step around here.

After the set, I took the kids to the side of the stage and met with Clyde for a few minutes, all of us sitting on metal chairs. He was a cheerful, gregarious man, seventy-eight years old, who'd been playing music most of his life. Clyde said he started playing mandolin and guitar at nine years old, and fiddle at fourteen, and western swing fiddle had always been his love. He said his main influences had been Cliff Brenner, JR Chatwell, and Johnny Gimble. "I had a lot of guys to listen to," he said. "And then I developed my own style."

Western swing, he said, involves melody, harmony, and improvising. "It's a version of jazz."

He said that western swing is at the top, in terms of the technical proficiency that it requires. Unlike bluegrass, he said, it's dance music, so it has to follow dance tempos, mostly Texas two-steps and waltzes.

"We're a dance band, more than a show band," he said. "When the floor's full, we're impressed."

I asked him what he thought would happen to western swing in the future, as generations and musical tastes change.

"The generation that loved that kind of music is dying out," he said. "Younger ones like it, but they don't get a chance to hear it."

Next up was the Playboys II, and I dragged the kids back to our seats, promising them this would be the last act we'd watch. Bob Wills's original band was called the Playboys, and this band had some of the original members. They were dapper-looking cowboys, wearing matching white shirts and blue ties. Johnny Gimble and Bob Boatright were their twin fiddlers, with Gimble, a well-known fiddler who had once played with Bob Wills himself, being the master of the afternoon. The Playboys II played "Deep Water" and "Sleepwalk" and then launched into an Indian-sounding dramatic rendition of "My Little Cherokee Maiden." As I listened, the bass player for the River Road Boys kept coming up to talk with me. It seemed he was flirting with me, but I tried to put him off.

"Are you coming Saturday to see Bobby Flores?" he asked, looking at me, and the kids, and then back at me. Sizing up my single-mom situation, I thought. "You know, I'll be playing with his band then."

"I might," I said.

"I played bass on some of the Playboys II albums," he said.

"Oh," I said. "Are any of them for sale over there?"

He ran over to check. There weren't any, he said. Too bad, I said. I tried to keep my eyes trained on the band. A few minutes later, he came back.

"You should really try to talk with Johnny Gimble," he said.

I assured him I would try.

"If you're looking for fiddle players, you have your hands full this weekend, that's for sure."

I nodded. "Sure do," I said.

The kids and I walked around again, watching the dancers, looking at the vendors selling turquoise jewelry and clingy western tops, while the band played "Sugar Moon" with Johnny and Bob doing twin fiddle solos. As the song wrapped up, I talked with a woman coming off the dance floor with her partner. She wore a bright flowered top and had short gray hair. I asked her why she liked western swing music.

"I like the social part," she said. She was sixty years old, and she had driven up from Abilene with her friends. They were staying in a camper in the parking lot.

"What else do you expect us old folks to do?" she said before grabbing the man with her and saying, "Come on, the next song's starting. Let's *dance!*"

∽⃝

The kids weren't really looking forward to the motel that I'd reserved for that night in Colorado City, so while we listened to the Playboys II, Rose and William drew red ink pictures in Rose's notebook of the motel's pool as they imagined it would be, with sharks and piranhas swimming in the water, and BEWARE OF THE POOL and DANGER signs all around. I laughed with them about it.

After the band finished, I went backstage with them to the dressing room to try to find Bob Boatright and Johnny Gimble. First I found Bob, who stood in the doorway and talked a few minutes. The sixty-eight-year-old, tall, unassuming fiddler said he'd been playing with the band for fifty-nine years, and he called western swing a combination of jazz and blues.

"It's a challenge," he said of western swing. "You never quit learning."

I asked him how he learned to play, and he said he depended on his ears.

"You need to stay in the chord progression and play what you feel," he said.

"So what's it like to play with Johnny Gimble?" I asked.

"It's great," he said. "He's one of the masters."

"Think you could get him to come out and talk with me?" I asked.

"Sure, I could try," he said. He went into the dressing room while the kids and I stood in the hallway, dodging band members in various states of dressing, undressing, and redressing, coming and going, buttoning western shirts, adjusting cowboy hats, carrying instrument cases. When Bob returned, he was slowly leading eighty-two-year-old Johnny Gimble over to me. Gimble moved with difficulty but had a firm handshake and a hard, strong look in his eyes. He told me he'd had several strokes a few years ago and felt lucky to still be playing. The first thing he tested when he came back from the hospital, he said, was whether he could still play fiddle. And he could.

I asked him how he defined western swing.

"It's jazz, you just play jazz," he said.

"How about improvising?" I asked. "How do you learn to do that?"

"Well, you need to be able to hum it," he said. "If you can't think it, you can't play it. And you play the chord progression. I like to hear a thread of melody through it so they know what song you're playing. My wife and I heard a player recently who improvised all over the place and totally lost the melody. I don't like that."

I liked his idea that to improvise well, you have to stay true to the melody. There seemed to be some truth to that, both for fiddle playing and for my own improvising of my life that I'd been doing lately. Keep some part of the melody going. Don't get totally lost.

"So what's going to happen to western swing?" I asked him.

"Well, we're going to die out, and it'll die, too," he said.

"Are you sure?" I asked. "What about the young ones coming up?"

"Yeah, well, there's lots of them coming to my fiddle camp," he admitted. "Some of them pretty good, too. So I guess there will be players as long as there are people to listen to them."

In addition to playing with the Playboys II, Gimble told me he played in a five-piece band called "Johnny Gimble and the Texas Swing Band," with his son Dick, a bass player.

"We play in a Mexican restaurant once a month on Congress Street in Austin," he said, glancing over at William, who'd been patiently waiting for me to finish so we could go on to the Days Inn and see if the pool was as bad as they imagined it to be.

"So do you play fiddle?" Gimble asked him.

"Yeah," William said. "A little, I guess."

Gimble asked what his favorite song was, and William said "Devil's Dream."

I joked that an old-time fiddler said to me one time when I played that for him that there were a lot of notes in that song.

Johnny laughed. "It reminds me of what someone said once: 'There's a lot of notes in that song, but they're not saying anything,'" he said.

I laughed, because fiddlers had told me something like that more than once over the past few months. It's the inflections, the phrasing, the style that make fiddle music come alive, not the notes.

He shook William's hand. "Keep playing," he said, looking hard at William. "Keep working at it."

"Thanks for taking the time to talk with me," I said.

"No problem," he said.

He autographed my notebook: "Thanx. Johnny Gimble."

I thanked him, and he walked slowly back into his dressing room.

When we left the music festival, we drove south toward Colorado City to find the dreaded motel. All the motels in Snyder had been booked long in advance, including the Best Western right by the Coliseum, so I'd been forced to reserve a place in the nearest town. As we drove, I was impressed by the red dirt fields, which looked like Martian landscapes. I kept thinking about Gillian Welch's song, "Red Clay Halo." At one point, I pulled over and took a picture of a field with a quarter moon over it. It looked like we were on Mars. A woman pulled over and said in a slow, kind Texas drawl, "Everything okay?"

"Sure," I said. "Thanks. Just taking a picture."

The kids made fun about that moment the rest of the trip; every time I'd stop to take a picture, they'd say, "She's taking pictures of fields again," or "Everything okay?" in a Texas drawl.

We made our way to Colorado City, but as soon as we drove into the motel's lot, William said he didn't want to stay there. Surveying the external corridors, the parking lot filled with pickup trucks, and the broken sign, I tended to agree with him. So I called the office on my cell phone and canceled our reservation, and using the AAA guidebook to the Southwestern states for the number, called ahead to a Holiday Inn Express. It was in Sweetwater, about twenty miles farther, and it turned out to be a newer hotel right on the highway. The trip had been one hotel after another, all of them basically the same. We could have been in Kansas or South Dakota or even Ohio, and every exit off every highway would look the same: same hotels, same restaurants, same Walmarts, same cars, same people. But by then we were exhausted, and the sameness of that Holiday Inn Express felt like home.

Sweetwater, we read on a little plaque in the hotel lobby, got its name from the fact that settlers built a town here on the only good, drinkable creek in the area. The rest of the water throughout the region was poisoned with gypsum, but Sweetwater had good water. So this is where we would stay for a few days. A place with good water.

On Friday, before heading back to the festival, I took the kids to Abilene. Abilene felt like a frontier town that had just been built, and I half-expected to see herds of cattle roaming the downtown area. We stopped in a museum called Frontier Texas! It featured a large, bronzed buffalo in front and told the history of this Western ranching town, and we also paid a visit to the Abilene Zoo. This peaceful zoo on the outskirts of town hosted only a few other visitors. Rose fed crackers to the giraffe, its long black tongue licking them from her hand. We looked at the small herd of American bison, trying to imagine what it must have been like when these large, brown animals roamed the plains. It wasn't hard to imagine, since Abilene had changed little over the years, and the plains still surrounded the town. It seemed that if the bison could just escape from the zoo, they'd feel at home in no time.

"I like this zoo," Rose said as we sat at a picnic table eating ice cream and watching the bison stand in the hot, dry heat. "It's peaceful."

"I agree," I said. "I could stay here all day."

We went to the gift shop and bought the requisite stuffed zoo animals, and then, despite the kids' protests, we drove the hour or so back to Snyder for another day at the western swing festival.

Back in Snyder, we stopped at a Dairy Queen near the Coliseum. The doors and tables were sticky, and flies buzzed through the air. A Mexican family sat around a large table in the middle. The kids ordered hot dogs and drinks, and we took the fare with us to the Coliseum, sitting at one of the tables by the concession stand. All the retirees sat around talking, taking a break between sets. Jake Hooker and the Outsiders, who I wanted to see, would be starting at 3 p.m.

At one table sat a healthy-looking, tanned couple in their sixties. I asked them if anyone was sitting across from them, and the man smiled and said, "You are!" So we sat down and struck up a conversation. They told me their names were Ed and Kathy, and they were from Albuquerque. They said they did all kinds of dancing: western swing, country, salsa. Kathy was a widow, and she said it took her a while to get back into dating. She met Ed through dancing, and now they went everywhere to dance together. They'd been coming to this festival and others for a while. They knew everyone around us, in fact. Through talking with them, I realized that what I saw as a random collection of RVing retirees was actually a community.

"See that woman over there, in the red shirt?" Kathy whispered to me. "She and her husband were the first to talk with me at one of these festivals. Now they're always coming up to me, asking how I am."

Then she pointed out another woman, probably in her seventies, at the end of the table. "And see her over there? We call her Queenie. She was in a wheelchair last year, but take a look at that. She's moved up to a walker now."

Kathy and Ed talked excitedly about their love of dance and the festival circuit.

While they talked, Rose struggled with her long hot dog from Dairy Queen, and I asked her if she needed help.

"Let her do it herself," said Ed good-naturedly. "Part of life is learning how to deal with things."

I smiled. "Yeah, I guess so," I said, realizing he was probably right.

After a few minutes, we heard Jake Hooker's band warming up onstage.

"Time to go do some dancing," Ed said, and they both waved good-bye. "See you on the dance floor!" they called back to us as they hurried inside. The kids and I made our way to the front, and passing the dance area we saw Ed and Kathy, already twirling and shuffling their way across the dance floor.

I was starting to feel at home at this festival, in the Coliseum with these people. Funny how after a few days in a place—west Texas, a Holiday Inn in Sweetwater, a western swing festival—you can start to feel at home. I promised the kids we'd just catch a few acts and then we'd leave. Reluctantly, they agreed.

Jake Hooker and his band had a honky-tonk flair. They were slick and polished, wearing black suits and cowboy hats. Jake played bass and sang, a lively presence in the middle of the stage. The fiddle player, Anthony Wilson, was tall and had a boyish face, and he looked over at Jake while they played. In between solos, he scrunched up his face as Jake talked.

The kids were bored, counting down the minutes to 4:15 when the set would finish. When it finally ended, I went on-stage with the kids and talked with Anthony, along with Randy Elmore, another fiddler helping him pack up. Randy had dark hair and a mustache, and he looked vaguely Latino. Anthony was tall and pale, with chewing tobacco—blackened teeth, wear-ing a black suit and a large white cowboy hat. Randy told me he'd been playing since 1965, when he was ten years old, taking lessons from Kenneth Pitts in Fort Worth. He learned country swing, polkas, "everything that's Texas fiddle." He talked about how western swing evolved from big band and Tommy Dorsey,

and how Bob Wills had been the major player behind that evolution. He also talked about how he had his own fiddle camp
each summer at Cisco Junior College. I told him I'd be going to
Mark O'Connor's fiddle camp in Tennessee in a few weeks, and
his eyes lit up.

"I'll be there, too," he said.

"So you'll be my teacher!" I said.

"Sure enough," he said. "I'll see you there."

"So what's going to happen with western swing?" I asked him.
"Is it going to stick around, or fade away?"

"Younger people like it when they hear it," he said. "But it's
hard to get the radio stations to pick it up. Most of the crowds are
fifty-five and over."

Anthony said he started playing when he was sixteen or seven-
teen. He came from a family of musicians and fiddle players, and
started his career by playing in contests.

"I wouldn't call myself a swing player," he told me, his boyish
face smiling shyly beneath his large cowboy hat.

"Why not?" I asked. "You sounded pretty good up there."

"He's just being modest," said Randy. "He plays swing."

"No, but I mean I play all types," said Anthony. "I'm a swing
player when I'm playing it, but that's not all I play."

"What about improvising?" I asked. "How do you do it?"

Randy echoed what Johnny Gimble had told me. "If you can
hear it in your head, then you can play it," he said.

"But what do you do when you find you can't go anywhere,
when you're too far off the melody?" I asked.

"That's part of the fun of improvising," said Randy. "Painting
yourself into a corner, and then getting out."

∞

The kids, by then agonizing in their requisite kid boredom by the side of the stage, were happy to finally leave. We drove for a while through Snyder. William took some photos of the Dairy Queen, the boarded-up gas stations, and Rose took a picture of a bronze buffalo on a downtown corner, in front of the Scurry County courthouse. Then we headed south again on 84, past red fields and many looming, twirling, large white windmills, the alternative electricity source of west Texas, fueled by the ever-present wind sweeping the plains. Back at the hotel we had snacks for dinner to eat up some of the food we'd collected on our trip. We were almost done with west Texas. The next day we'd head up to Lubbock and catch a plane back to Columbus.

I was proud of the kids, and of myself. Proud to have found some western swing fiddlers, to have learned something of their culture. Proud to have survived the long journey through vast deserts, with William reading the maps and guidebooks and Rose watching her DVDs. Proud they had put up with their mom on an ill-advised, cross-country trip. Proud to find Holiday Inn Expresses where necessary, and to have adapted to many different environments. I thought that night about what all those fiddlers had been saying about improvising—hearing it in your head, keeping track of the melody, trying to paint yourself into a corner just for the fun of it—and it finally began to hit home. I was improvising.

Chapter 13

On the Wildcat Trail
Fiddle Camp

At the Nashville airport on a Saturday afternoon a few weeks later, I got off the plane carrying my trusty violin. No, my *fiddle*. I made my way to the Hertz counter, where I signed paperwork, presented my credit card, and picked up a map of Tennessee. On the lot outside, I picked up a 2008 red Hyundai Elantra with XM satellite radio. After studying the map for a minute, I maneuvered my way out of the lot and onto Interstate 40 going west. It was pouring rain, and I turned the windshield wipers up as fast as they would go to keep up with the onslaught. I was going to Montgomery Bell State Park, where the annual Mark O'Connor fiddle camp is held. As I drove west, the rain and thunder dissipated. I was tired, spent, and numb. I just needed to get to the fiddle camp.

Ever since I'd heard about the Mark O'Connor fiddle camp from Darrell Murray, I knew it was something I wanted to try. So I left the kids with their grandparents, since their dad didn't have room in his small apartment to put them up, and left for

Nashville. I also made plans to spend a few weeks after the camp driving on to Louisiana, exploring, seeing what I could find.

I felt guilty leaving the kids, but I knew I needed to take this trip if I was going to be anything like a good mom. I needed to get away. I needed to travel. I needed to make sense of my life as a soon-to-be single mom before going back to it. I still felt shaky, not quite able to function without taking a daily dose of Xanax. At home after our southwest trip, the dirty laundry had been piling up, and I'd been feeding the kids cheese and crackers for dinner every night. They were having to fold their own clothes, make their own beds, and keep themselves occupied more than before, and I knew they were eyeing me, wondering if their mom was going to make it.

And, honestly, I didn't know myself.

Perhaps, I thought, a couple more weeks of adventure would help propel me into the future. I looked forward to hanging out with fiddlers, with finally having some intense, serious instruction in fiddling. It was time for me to not just listen to fiddling, but to *play* it.

Montgomery Bell is a reclaimed natural landmark, a place where iron had been mined and forged in the early nineteenth century. General James Robertson, sometimes called the father of Tennessee, started the Cumberland Iron Works in this part of the state in 1795. Later, Montgomery Bell came from Pennsylvania to operate the iron furnace, eventually buying it. Over time, the iron works dwindled, leaving behind pieces of iron and slag, old furnaces, and the foundations of pioneer homes. The forest grew back, trees replacing ore pits and houses. In the 1930s, the state park was founded, and many of the park's cabins and other buildings were built by CCC workers. Thick woods now cover the park, which also has lakes, an inn, a golf course, and a campground that serves as the site for the fiddle camp.

After the long trip through the Southwest with the kids, I missed having them around. The drive from Nashville felt quiet and lonely with no one in the front seat reading a map and no one in the backseat watching a movie. I realized how much I'd been leaning on them for a sense of reality, a sense of purpose.

At the park, I checked into the inn, a six-story building nestled into one of the park's rocky hillsides. I found my room, and then I went back to the car to get my suitcase and violin. As I walked in, a woman and her husband saw me carrying my case.

"Are you going to play some music for us tonight?" she asked.

"No, I'm here for a fiddle camp," I said.

"Oh, well, that's exciting," she said, and I nodded, hurrying up to my room—number 515—where I put my suitcase and violin on the bed. Famished, I went down to the dining room for dinner. I stood in the buffet line for salad, catfish, hushpuppies, and corn, sat down and ate it all, and then went back for more. After hitting the line three times, I went back to my room and collapsed—my fiddle and suitcase on one bed and me on the other. The next morning, I strolled onto my little balcony and looked at Lake Acorn, watching kids paddle around in canoes and bass fishermen on wooden bridges casting into the peaceful waters. Rose, I thought, would really like to come to this park and rent a boat with me. After breakfast, I ran along a rocky, poison ivy–laced trail, which had a sign announcing it as the Wildcat Trail, up past a dam and a stream, down to the camp office, and back. I felt alone and alive on that trail. I thought: *This is exactly where I need to be right now. On the Wildcat Trail.*

After lunch, I drove over to the fiddle camp area in the

Group I campground, following the little white wooden signs shaped like fiddles along the side of the road. The park ranger outside the camp area told me that today I could drive in and park near the registration area, but for the rest of the week I'd have to park on the grass and walk in with my fiddle to the camp. Some people stayed in cabins around the fiddle camp area, but people like me, who stayed at the inn, had to park and walk in. Two women sat at a table registering people as they arrived. A woman with shoulder-length silver hair found my name on the list, crossed me off, and handed me a blue lanyard and a badge that read MARK O'CONNOR FIDDLE CAMP, VIVIAN WAGNER, OHIO, FIDDLER.

It made me happy to be called a fiddler.

"Just make sure to always wear your lanyard," the woman told me. "Dinner's at six in this building here, and at eight there's an orientation at the covered pavilion over there. Make sure to bring your fiddle, since there's a fiddle jam after the orientation."

She told me I'd been placed in Level C, which meant Intermediate, age eighteen and up. Intermediate meant "At least two years of instruction. Know less than twenty fiddle tunes, can learn by ear but have no experience with improvisation." It sounded about right.

She also gave me a green mug emblazoned with the fiddle camp's logo. I was told to always bring my mug to mealtimes, since I'd use it for my drinks. By the porch, a couple of guys were unloading food from a van with THE MAD PLATTER painted on its side.

"Thanks," I said, standing awkwardly by the table for a few minutes. It wasn't like I was going to meet anyone I knew, but I thought maybe I'd find someone to talk with. Everyone seemed busy checking in and unloading, though. It felt like my first day in a new school. After a while, I left and drove back to the inn. In my room, I studied the camp's daunting schedule. That night, there would be dinner at 6, and the orientation and fiddle jam at 8. The first two days of the camp involved breakfast from 8 to 9, and then something called a "Fiddler's Shuffle" all day until 5:30. This meant that my group and I would cycle through all the different instructors in ninety-minute blocks, giving us a chance to get to know the style, genre, and method of each instructor. The last three days of the camp we would choose which instructors' workshops to attend. Each night at 7:30 there would be concerts of the instructors, and on Friday night there would be a concert for students. Basically, it looked like I'd be fiddling all the time in a whirlwind of activity straight through the week.

I couldn't wait to begin.

That night at dinner I ate at the wooden table with a motley assortment of fiddlers. An elementary school strings teacher from Georgia. A family from Texas with their twin fiddling sons. A woman who had been a computer programmer for the army in Germany and was now turning to music, studying fiddle and music technology at Georgia Tech. A woman from Baltimore who worked as a science writer for the National Institutes of Health, at the camp as a guardian for her nine-year-old fiddling daughter. A woman from the mountains of Georgia who did medical sonographs and was teaching herself to play fiddle. Everyone taking new directions, learning new things, finding new paths in life. All through the fiddle.

After dinner, we made our way out to the covered pavilion, where there would be an orientation at 8 p.m. The man giving the orientation told us not to sit on the ground, otherwise we'd get chiggers; not to swim in the nearby lake, because there were dangerous snakes; not to bring alcohol, drugs, and firearms into the park. He brought out a long metal hook and said, "There's a student concert on Friday night, as you all know if you read the schedule. If you play longer than two minutes, we'll use this on you." Everyone laughed nervously. A father sitting by his daughter to my left said, "They've never used that before. Don't worry."

After the orientation, we launched into the fiddle jam. Everyone got out their fiddles, two guitarists sat in the middle of a semicircle, and we began playing tunes. A person would start playing a tune, the guitarists would pick it up, and it would spread through the group. Some people played backup, and others who knew the tune played along. Some I recognized, like "Arkansas Traveler" and "Devil's Dream," and I joined in. Others, like "Jerusalem Road" and "Wednesday Night Waltz," I didn't know, but after a few repetitions I was able to jump in and play along. And sometimes I found myself playing harmony and improvising without even realizing it.

As I played in that darkening Tennessee night with the group of fiddle players, I started to think: *My badge is right. I'm a fiddler. Maybe I'm able to do this after all.*

The next morning, I woke up early and sat on the deck looking over the lake. I thought again about how the kids would like it here, how Rose would love the canoes and the lake, how William would enjoy the fiddle classes. All this self-exploration was fine, but the fact was, I missed the kids.

I looked again through my registration materials and schedule. I needed to decide if Group C—Intermediate, ages 18 and up—was the right group for me. I was torn between that group and Group D—Intermediate Classical—for players who "have had classical instruction but very little fiddle instruction. Have not had much experience learning by ear or improvising. Do not know many fiddle tunes." That last requirement tripped me up, since I knew a few fiddle tunes, at least from my fiddle books, and I knew my way around fiddle music. So I decided to stay in Group C.

I loaded myself and my violin into the car again and drove over to the camp, past the golf course and up the road that would become familiar to me over the course of the week. I parked and walked up the road to the main cabin for breakfast. All the campers, kids and adults, had piled their fiddles around the front porch of the cabin, and I did the same before opening the screen door into the breakfast area. It was filled with noise, plates clanking, people talking, and the smell of camp breakfast, which immediately brought me back to those days at Arrowbear Music Camp, where we'd have early morning breakfasts in the woods much like this one before going to practice in orchestras and chamber ensembles. I filled up my Mark O'Connor fiddle camp green mug with coffee, got my pancakes and fruit, and dug in. I sat at a table without knowing anyone's names yet, and we talked about fiddling, about our thoughts about the camp, about where we were from.

Before long, it was time to clear our plates and head over to the morning orientation, where O'Connor himself welcomed us. He said to go into the first day with an open mind about what kind of fiddling we wanted to do, and what teachers we wanted to work with.

"It might change as you go through the shuffle," he told us. "Because there are so many new things to see and learn."

We met Helen and Jim, some of the camp's administrative staff, and Mark introduced each of the instructors. He emphasized the camp's spirit of crossover, hybridity, and cross-pollination.

"One of the things that distinguishes our camp is that it breaks down all the barriers between types of fiddling," he told us. I loved the idea of different fiddle styles informing each other, influencing each other, cross-pollinating.

Fiddle camp was a five-day rush of classes, tunes, teachers, styles, notes, ornamentations, double-stops, and chops. I and my group learned Irish and Cape Breton versions of "Temperance Reel." We were introduced to the Swedish folk group Väsen and learned a haunting melody called "Dragonship" from violinist Darol Anger. We studied jazz violin and improvisation with John Blake and Tracy Silverman, and old-time fiddling with Bruce Molsky. We collected tunes like butterflies: a hybridized combination of old-time tunes like "Sally Gooden" and "Wild Horses in the Canebrake"; Texas tunes like "Southwest Swing"; pop tunes like "Slow Boat to China"; and bluegrass tunes like "Paddy on the Turnpike." It was almost more than one fiddler could bear, but I devoured every last bit, recording, making notes, trying to remember everything I could.

O'Connor taught just one class, in which he told us his theory of fiddle music, and of the camp itself. He talked more about cross-pollination and what he called the "edge effect," how bringing together fiddlers and violinists from different traditions offers the possibility of creating some entirely new, unexpected, transformational music. He compared going through different phases in life to experiencing different vistas and environments. I knew what he meant. It felt like every class had a little nugget of wisdom that related not just to my fiddling, but to my mixed-up personal life, and I was collecting them and saving them for later.

Over the course of the week, I got to know the other members of my group—a soft-spoken young man with longish hair named Adam, who had driven all the way from Maine with his brother to attend the camp. And Rhonda, a thin, jeans-wearing woman in her forties from Georgia who I'd met at the orientation the day before and begun to befriend. She had shoulder-length brownish red hair, and she worked as an ultrasound specialist. She was just learning to play fiddle, from books and DVDs, so she admitted to feeling self-conscious at the camp, uncertain of herself and her talent or abilities. But she had a quiet ambition or drive that I admired. And there was Amber, a massage therapist, also from Georgia. She had long, curly hair and an air of certainty and intelligence and calmness about her. These fellow campers became my tribe. I also met a fiddle player from Cleveland named Jennifer O'Neal. She had short hair and a thin frame, a string teacher in a Cleveland school district who played fiddle on the side. She told me she'd recorded a few albums and that she used to have a band called Woodshed Mercy, but now she did mostly solo and recording work for various bands. She told me about a few venues she plays in around Cleveland, places with names like the Barking Spider and the Town Fryer. She seemed way beyond me, well versed in the world of fiddling and performing. She was also in the advanced group, which made sense. I looked up to her.

Perhaps the oddest class of the week was one I took with a Russian classical violinist named Anastasia Khitruk, a thin, graceful young woman with long, reddish blond, flowing curly hair who also proved to be a hard taskmaster. In the class, she asked for volunteers from our group, and a young man got up and played first a Telemann and then a Mozart piece for her. She watched, coolly, assessing his talent, his skill, his tone. At one point, she wanted him to play lighter, more like Mozart, so she told him to dance while he played, and then she danced with him, bobbing up and down on her ballet feet while he struggled to dance and play at the same time. At another, she told him to imagine he was a girl, winking and flirting while he played. And though he clearly felt uncomfortable he obeyed that demand. And sure enough, his playing became lighter, more free. As the dusty sun shown in through the cabin's windows, it lit up Khitruk's hair and face, and I found myself imagining her own childhood lessons with some difficult teacher in Russia. As I watched her, I wondered: *What is a classical violinist doing here at fiddle camp? Isn't her cool, calculated judgment one of the things I wanted to escape by taking up fiddle?* But at the same time, her sharp tongue, and her wit, entranced me. Her fastidiousness was something missing, perhaps, from the other classes here. Her insistence on good tone and pitch something foreign to many fiddle players.

Rhonda volunteered to go next, and I thought about how brave she was. She stood with Khitruk and played one of her fiddle tunes. By the end of her performance, she was shaking, but she had done it. And Khitruk was surprisingly compassionate with her, focusing not on wrong notes or questionable tone, but on her demeanor, on her need to be forceful. When Rhonda walked back to her seat, I smiled and gave her a thumbs up, and she smiled back. She had done it.

Then, strangely, Khitruk told our class something that sounded kind of fiddle-like. "You all have a journey you will be on," she told us. "The journey is important, too. Sometimes the wrong note is perfect. You have to allow yourself to make mistakes."

At times in this whirl of classes, I felt like the lessons were aimed specifically at me and my situation. Like when Anger gave us a brief theory lesson, playing for us a "flat fifth," calling it a "note of tension, unhappiness, or potential unhappiness, which might resolve to happiness, or at least we want it to," and showing how to resolve it. At these moments, the pace of the camp slowed, and I could see what was happening in clearer relief.

I was here to learn not just how to play fiddle, but how to live my life.

∽

At the end of each day, I returned to my room at the inn exhausted and spent. I'd go through all of the music, trying to make sense of everything I'd learned so far. I'd sit on the deck and look over the little lake. I'd call the kids.

"How is the camp going?" William asked me one night.

"It's a lot of work," I told him. "It's kind of like school. I'm going to lots of different workshops, learning different tunes, learning how to improvise."

"Oh," he said, sounding faraway.

"Next summer, maybe I can bring you here," I said, suddenly missing him and Rose. "There are lots of kids here, and I think you'd like it."

"Yeah," he said. "That might be fun."

∽

One day, midweek, I lost track of Rhonda until lunch. When I caught up with her, I could tell something was wrong.

"Is everything okay?" I asked her.

She shook her head. "I've spent all morning crying," she said. "I'm just not getting it. I'm not able to do this."

"What do you mean?" I asked.

"It's just too hard," she said. "No matter how hard I try, I just can't do it."

I gave her a hug, trying to comfort her. "You could try going to the beginning workshops," I said.

She nodded and looked down at her plate. "Yeah," she said. "I guess I might do that. I'm going to just keep trying, though. I'm going to keep practicing."

In the end, she decided to stick with our group and not descend to the beginner's level. I admired her drive to succeed, her will to master this difficult, complicated instrument, her desire to make some progress despite all odds, among much more accomplished fiddlers. I felt the same way. Even though I knew the notes, I had a hard time keeping up with all the styles, all the tunes, all the possible directions. We had too much to absorb, too much to learn.

The week culminated in a concert by campers, and as I attended workshops, I decided to do two different performances at this final concert. One would be "Southwest Swing," which we'd play as a twin fiddle tune. Jennifer, the fiddler and strings teacher from Cleveland, and I asked Randy Elmore to teach us how to play twin fiddle, and he spent one whole workshop teaching us how to play "Southwest Swing" in thirds. He played through the tune with a young fiddler who was one of the stars of the camp, and then he taught it to us phrase by phrase, first the lower part, and then the upper part. Jennifer and I were happy; this would be our tune. We practiced it separately for a couple of days, and then we set aside time to practice together in shady areas under trees at the campground, before dinner, after lunch, whenever we could spare a few minutes. It was fun learning twin fiddling, a collaborative effort. We didn't have any music written down, since we'd learned it just by ear, so as we practiced we worked on simply learning the notes. Once we got those down, we recorded ourselves playing to see how we sounded as a duet. At our best moments we sounded perfect, like one violin, swinging and swaying away.

The second tune I'd play at the performance was one called "Sourwood Mountain," which we learned on Friday morning from Bruce Molsky's class on singing and fiddling. He taught us the tune, which involved singing while playing double-stops on our fiddles.

"When you sing it, you swing it," he said. "When you play it off a piece of paper, you play it more methodically. Music is about speech."

Still, though, he thought we needed help with the words, so he passed out a photocopied sheet that had them printed on it:

> *Chickens crowing on Sourwood Mountain,*
> *Call up your dogs and let's go a-huntin'.*
> *Hey ho diddle um-a-day.*
>
> *My love lives in the head of the holler.*
> *She won't come and I won't foller.*
> *Hey ho diddle um-a-day.*
>
> *Say old man, I want your daughter.*
> *Wash my dishes and carry my water.*
> *Hey ho diddle um-a-day.*

Fifteen cents a dollar and a quarter,
Say, old man, I'll take her if you want her.
Hey ho diddle um-a-day.

My true love is a blue-eyed daisy.
If I don't get her, I'll go crazy.
Hey ho diddle um-a-day.

If my love is across the ocean,
I'd go see her if I took a notion.
Hey ho diddle um-a-day.

As the class wrapped up, one woman named Chris and I kept playing the tune and singing it, really getting into it. We went through it several times, trying to catch all the notes and double-stops, and trying to master singing while playing.

"Maybe we should play this in the concert," I said.

"Well, okay," she said. "Let's do it!"

Chris and I just had a few hours before the concert, so we set a time to meet after dinner to practice. I worked on the vocal harmony, and we sawed through the piece as many times as we could before the concert began.

That Friday night, tension and expectation hung in the air as we neared the concert time. I started getting nervous, my hands shaking and sweating, my heart pounding, so I took a Xanax out of my purse and downed it with a swig of water from my camp cup. I felt comfortable with the "Southwest Swing," since Jennifer and I had had a few days to work on it and let it percolate through our consciousness. But I'd just learned "Sourwood Mountain" and was afraid I wouldn't even remember the tune.

I found an old oak tree out of hearing distance of the pavilion, where the concert was taking place. There I played through "Sourwood Mountain" again and again, the Xanax spreading through my system, the night dark, the stars twinkling overhead, the cicadas buzzing in the forest surrounding me. And as I played, I entered a rhythmic, meditative state, feeling one with the forest, the campground, and "Sourwood Mountain." It felt like I was on Sourwood Mountain, or at least near it. The moon hung overhead, and in the distance I could hear the sawing and melodies of fiddles playing under the lighted pavilion. The forest and the damp, hot Tennessee night listened as I played and sang, and after a few more times through the tune, I felt ready for the performance. I went back to the pavilion, found Chris and Jennifer, and we awaited our turn. We were near the end of the concert, since we had signed our names on the sign-up sheet late. We were numbers 55 and 56 in the lineup, just a few short of the end, so we wouldn't be up until after 10 p.m.

Finally, our time came. Jennifer and I were first. She had asked Daniel Carwile to accompany us on guitar, and he graciously agreed. Our performance went well, with its smooth harmony, and we each made only a few mistakes. People clapped, and then Chris and I played "Sourwood Mountain." It wasn't perfect, but it went okay. Afterward, Bruce, who stood behind the stage, told us we had been brave to play something we'd just learned that morning. He said the harmony and the call-and-response style we used for the song worked.

I hugged Jennifer, and then Chris. I was proud. I'd played in my first fiddle concert, and it had gone okay. I felt like a real fiddler, or at least someone who could get up and play a few tunes for an audience, which was definitely more than I could do before. I'd played in plenty of orchestra concerts, but standing up and playing tunes I'd learned only a few days previously in front of an audience of fiddlers in an outside pavilion was new for me. And I'd done it. I drove back to the inn, collapsed on the bed, and slept more soundly than I had in weeks.

∽◯

In the morning, I packed my bags and drove over for the last breakfast, eating pancakes with strawberries and saying good-byes.

"I have something for you," Jennifer said, pulling out two CDs of her band, Woodshed Mercy. "Which one do you want?"

I looked at them. "Both?" I asked.

She smiled. "Sure, you can have them. I wasn't sure you'd want both, but you can have them."

"Thanks so much," I said. "Let's keep in touch."

She nodded. I said good-bye to Adam and Isaac, who would set off for Maine that day, and to Amber and her husband, and to Rhonda. We would all be getting in our cars and heading to our separate states, but we'd bonded, sharing this one difficult, overwhelming, magical week in the Tennessee woods.

"Are you coming to fiddle camp next year?" I asked Adam and Isaac.

"We might," Adam said. "How about you?"

"I'm thinking about it," I said. "I might bring my son. I think he would like it."

"Well, if you're ever in Maine, stop on by and we'll play some tunes," he said.

"I'd like that," I said. "I really would."

I hugged them both, and traded e-mail addresses and phone numbers, promised to write, to keep in touch, to see each other at future fiddle camps. Here were people that a week before I'd never met, and now they were good friends. Bonding happens with the shared experiences, the shared hardships, the shared learning.

I got back in my little red rental car and headed out, through the park entrance, on the country roads, and back onto the interstate. My mind full of tunes, my fiddle stowed behind my seat, and the sun shining, I felt slightly stronger than I had a week before. As if I were getting somewhere. The fiddle lessons had fortified me, given me a sense that I would be able to survive, I would be able to improvise into the future. The sun shining, the green rolling Tennessee hills passing by, I turned the satellite radio to a bluegrass station and headed south.

Chapter 14

Survival and Recovery
Cajun Fiddle After Katrina

Just across the Louisiana border, I pulled over at a rest stop and called Jonno Frishberg, a Cajun fiddler I'd found on the Internet a few weeks earlier. I'd e-mailed him, telling him I wanted to learn about Cajun fiddling, and he said he'd love to meet me. On the phone now at the rest stop, he told me he'd be playing that night at a restaurant in downtown New Orleans, Mulate's, and that I'd be welcome to come on by. Maybe, he said, we could also meet for breakfast the next morning. His voice sounded kind and reassuring. I wondered, briefly, why I was calling a man I'd never met and agreeing to go to a restaurant to see him play, and possibly to meet him in the morning. It felt right, though. Something I needed to do.

Getting back on the road toward New Orleans, heading south through the state, the trees got shorter, the land got swampier, and I felt myself nearing water. I began watching for signs of Hurricane Katrina, which had swept through three years before, but at first I saw nothing other than swamplands. Then, suddenly and unexpectedly, I came across acres upon acres of small white FEMA trailers, in rows by the interstate. It was my first glimpse of the disaster's aftermath. I got off the highway at the exit by the trailers, bought gas, and took pictures of the deserted trailers. I knew I was entering a ravaged land; I could feel it in the air. Then I got back on the interstate. It was getting late in the day, and I wanted to make it to New Orleans in time to catch Jonno's show at Mulate's.

As I neared the city, I could smell the ocean. Along the eastern edge of New Orleans, I began to see houses that had been blasted and torn by the hurricane's winds and flooding, still in various stages of disrepair and repair. I saw roofs still covered with blue tarp and boarded-up apartment buildings. I passed block after block of decimated neighborhoods, and I knew I was only seeing the surface of the damage, that it was impossible to understand its full scope hurtling by on the interstate.

Strangely, amid all the devastation, I saw a Home Depot, shiny and brightly lit among the ruined neighborhoods in the early evening light. Home Depot, apparently, had been doing pretty brisk business as people struggled to rebuild their lives and homes.

My main mental images of New Orleans were from the news during and after Hurricane Katrina, the city flooded, the people desperate. Water up to the roofs of houses. I had no idea what to expect in person. In the three years since the disaster, New Orleans had fallen from the news, except for occasional reports of its rising crime.

Still listening to the bluegrass satellite radio station, I drove in on Highway 10 over Lake Pontchartrain in the early evening, the sun setting over the lake, the sky pale blue and pink. As I drove into the network of roads and highways and cloverleaf interchanges near the downtown area, I passed the Super Dome, that building that had been a central gathering place for people escaping the floodwaters in Katrina's aftermath. Now it looked clean, well kept, as if nothing had happened. I followed my Map-Quest directions to the Hampton Inn and Suites, across from the Convention Center, which had been another emergency staging area for flood victims. The downtown seemed eerily quiet; it rested on relatively high ground. In a city that had been 80 percent under water in the days following Hurricane Katrina, this was part of the 20 percent that had escaped major flooding.

I checked into my hotel room, a king suite, at the Hampton Inn, which occupied a renovated brick warehouse. My room had tall painted brick walls and posters of old prints of pineapples and palm trees, along with French-looking furniture and a high double bed with a cream-colored comforter. It felt luxurious, the most luxurious hotel room I'd ever been in, here in a city that just three years earlier had suffered almost complete devastation.

Settling in, I called the kids at their grandparents' house. Rose asked immediately about the room; she always likes to hear about hotels.

"I have a dishwasher and real dishes and silverware," I told her.

"Wow," she said. "What else?"

"A tall bed, and a really high ceiling," I said. "It's beautiful."

"That sounds nice," she said. "I wish I was there."

"I know, honey," I told her. "I wish you were, too."

When William got on the phone, I told him I was in New Orleans.

"You *are?*" he asked, incredulous. "Where Hurricane Katrina was?"

"Yes, that New Orleans," I said.

"Is it all gone now?" he asked.

"Yes," I said. "Though I saw a lot of ruined houses on the way. Right around where I am it seems okay."

I talked briefly with Sherry, who sounded faintly worried about me being in New Orleans by myself. New Orleans, post-Katrina, has a reputation as being a crime-ridden, dangerous city. I'd been a little scared to go there, too, wondering if it would be safe to wander about the streets. But I told her it seemed safe enough in the downtown area, and that I had plans to meet with a Cajun fiddler.

I freshened up and got ready to go find Mulate's, which according to the city map was just down the street from my hotel. I changed clothes, washed my face, and took the elevator down to the main level. I stopped at the front desk and asked the young man, who had blond hair and a smooth face, if he could point me to Mulate's.

The clerk pulled out a little hotel map of the city.

"See, we're here, and Mulate's is just two blocks down," he said, pointing at the map. He had a lilting, sweet voice and old-money, old–New Orleans charm.

"Thanks," I said. "Do you think it's safe for me to walk around?"

He smiled and nodded. "Yeah, it's completely safe," he said.

"So was this area flooded?" I asked him.

"No, this small part wasn't, this and the French Quarter," he said. "And a few other neighborhoods, wherever people were smart enough to build high."

He took out a pen and drew some lines and circles on the map.

"This was flooded, here," he said. "And here, and here. There were only a few places that didn't get much water. I know what people say about New Orleans, how it shouldn't be built below sea level. I love my city, though, and there are smart ways to build it up again. You just need to build high."

After a while, he bid me good night, and I headed out onto the street.

∞

Cajun music has its origins in the French Acadian settlers who came to Louisiana after they were expelled from Acadie, or Nova Scotia, in 1755. It had been French folk music, but it evolved when it came into contact with British immigrants, and it transformed even further in nineteenth-century Louisiana when it intersected with African beats, blues, Spanish songs, and the improvisational singing of southwestern Louisiana's Native Americans.

Cajun music developed to include a heady mix of French, Spanish, and British dance tunes, including contradanses, gigues, galops, reels, mazurkas, polkas, cotillions, valses Julien, valses a deux temps, and Varsouviennes. The fiddle was a standard instrument for Cajuns, and in the late nineteenth century, German immigrants introduced the accordion, a loud and raucous instrument good for being heard at wild and wooly Cajun dances. Cajun fiddling and accordion playing evolved together, each instrument echoing and shaping the other.

In the early twentieth century, musicians started to make the first recordings of traditional Cajun music, such as "Allons à Lafayette," recorded in 1928 by Joe and Cleoma Falcon. Amédé Ardoin and Dennis McGeen made another early recording in 1929, with "Two Step de Eunice," "Madame Atchen," and "La Valse à Abe." The recordings of Cajun music led to a broader audience, and also the introduction of new influences, including jazz, swing, and rock. New generations of musicians took it up, and Cajun music gradually made its way into mass culture.

Cajun music, in other words, embodies a history of change, evolution, and improvisation, much like other fiddle music. Through centuries of backwoods and swamp dances, the music, like a living thing, had grown and survived.

Out on the street that night, only a few people walked by on the sidewalk, mostly people from a food and beverage convention being held at the convention center across the street. I could identify them by their name tags. I walked past a small park, which had a memorial to Hurricane Katrina and its survivors, and then past a newsstand and a pharmacy. A few blocks down, I saw Mulate's on the corner of Julia Street and Convention Boulevard.

A tan building with light green trim, it sported a red sign saying WORLD FAMOUS MULATE'S, THE ORIGINAL CAJUN RESTAURANT. Going through the wooden doors, I found myself in a swirl of music, people, and warmth. The air smelled thick with Cajun spices, and waiters hurried by holding plates of bread, shrimp, and blackened fish. Jonno and his band, Bayou DeVille, were playing on a stage on the far end of the restaurant, on the other side of a dance floor, where old ladies, small children, and middle-aged couples twirled to the music. I made my way through the crowd, over to the stage, where I listened to the band for a while. I made eye contact with Jonno, smiling. He smiled back, while sawing away on his fiddle and singing in French, often at the same time. Tall, with close-cropped, blondish brown hair, he wore a button-down denim shirt, and when he sang, he held his fiddle, with an electric pickup connected to an amp, down on his arm by his chest. The band had one other fiddler, a young boy playing bass, and a young woman playing guitar.

The restaurant had been designed for just such entertainment. Behind the band on the stage, a large, brightly colored painting displayed a fiddler and the name "Mulate's." The restaurant had a lively, raucous, and colorful atmosphere. I read in the brochure for the restaurant that it had been closed for eight months after Katrina, and during that time it had been looted. It reopened, however, and now it offered live music and dancing every night, mostly for tourists but also for the city's residents. I picked up a few of the CDs the band had stacked along a shelf in front of the stage, and Jonno smiled and motioned that I could have them. "Thanks," I mouthed, looking at the CDs, one of which had on its cover a beautiful painting of houses floating, and I knew this must have been a post-Katrina CD.

After a while, I made my way over to the bar, where I ordered blackened oysters, bread, and butter. I sopped up every last bit of the dish's lovely, spicy sauce with my bread, listening to the waltzes and two-steps of Bayou DeVille.

The next day, I got up, worked out in the hotel exercise room, and ate breakfast in the regal dining room, watching food and beverage conference attendees talking on their cell phones and planning their days over bowls of cereal and half grapefruits. Once back in the room, I called Jonno, and when he didn't answer I left a message, wondering if he'd still want to meet me that morning. A few minutes later he called back.

"Just fixing the tire on my van," he said, sounding resourceful and confident. These people in New Orleans seemed able to do just about anything: survive floods, play music, fix tires. Just the kind of people I wanted to get to know.

"Would you like to meet somewhere, or should I just drive over to your house?" I asked, surprised again to be inviting myself to the home of a stranger. In my prior life, I would never have done something like that. But now it seemed perfectly normal, and Jonno answered graciously.

"Sure, come on over," he said. "The kids are still asleep, and Maria's off meditating."

He gave me directions to his house. I drove a few minutes east of downtown on the interstate to an exit called Elysian Fields. I stayed on the divided boulevard going north and then turned right on Gentilly Boulevard, making my way to the neighborhood of Gentilly Ridge. I drove by small one-story houses with a brown high waterline still on their white stucco, run-down yards with tall grass, boarded-up windows, and roofs with the distinctive blue tarp that dots neighborhoods throughout New Orleans. I turned down a quiet residential boulevard, passed Music Street, and turned left on Arts Street, thinking that only in New Orleans would streets have such names.

I noticed right away that Jonno's block itself had been spared the worst water levels. A few houses were undergoing repairs and renovations, but mostly it looked like a quiet suburban street with nice, solid arts-and-crafts-style homes. I stopped in front of Jonno's yellow house, which had flowers out front and prayer flags strung across the porch, flapping in the early-morning breeze. I parked my car, reached to the backseat to get my violin, and walked up to his front door.

"You made it," he called out, opening the screen door and welcoming me inside with one hand, holding a cup of coffee with another. He seemed relaxed, in jeans and a loose shirt. "Come on in."

"I made it to Arts Street," I said. "It's a beautiful neighborhood, and a lovely house."

"Thanks," he said. "Care for a cup of coffee?"

"Sure," I said. "Thanks."

I sat at the dining room table, feeling comfortable and happy, protected, slightly aware of the irony in the fact that I'd come to New Orleans to meet with people still trying to rebuild their lives, and *I* was leaning on *them* for support and sustenance, not the other way around.

He got me a cup of coffee, and we sat at the wooden table in the dining room with the midmorning Sunday sun streaming in the windows. We talked about the concert the night before at Mulate's, and he told me that his neighbors had been having a birthday party there, which made it a special evening. I asked him who the bass player and guitarist were, and he said they were his kids, Colin and Eva.

Jonno said he began playing violin in fourth grade, while growing up near Washington, D.C. Mostly, he played classical music in the school orchestra, but in high school he played what he called "rock viola" in a few garage bands. He hadn't had much exposure to fiddle music, though. At nineteen, in 1979, he headed down to Louisiana to work in Lafayette's oil fields. His mom told him he might want to check out Cajun music and fiddle while he was down there. She sent his violin down to him, and he began to teach himself fiddle music from books like *1,000 Fiddle Tunes.*

"I was trying to teach myself in a vacuum," Jonno said.

One day he went to a music store and bought some cassettes

of Cajun music. He listened to them over and over, trying to get a handle on this music. Most of his friends in southwestern Louisiana at the time listened to Lynyrd Skynyrd and Fleetwood Mac; they considered Cajun music old-fashioned. But he started going to small shows, collecting music, and taking lessons when he could from the old guys.

"I learned a few waltzes on my own," he said. "I played, and I learned it on the fly."

In 1986, he put together a "psychedelic Cajun band," Mamou, which did some touring. He met his wife, Maria, while playing at a bar with this band in Buffalo, New York, and they got married and settled in New Orleans. He played in a few other bands, learning more about Cajun music as he went. He said that over time he learned a set of mother tunes that keep cropping up again and again in Cajun music. He perfected his style and his repertoire until, finally, the oil field worker who had played Suzuki violin as a child had become a Cajun fiddler.

After a few minutes, our conversation turned to the elephant in every New Orleans room: Hurricane Katrina.

"Did you get water?" I asked, aware of an odd combination of prurience, concern, and curiosity behind my question.

"Just to the top step of the porch," he said. "We came within inches of losing everything to the water."

Gentilly Ridge, he explained, much as the hotel clerk had done with me the preceding night, is slightly higher than the surrounding Gentilly area, and this height made all the difference. It explained why I saw ruined houses driving in, but then as I made it to Arts Street the damage looked less severe.

Jonno said that when Katrina bore down on Louisiana, Maria thought maybe they could wait it out. They'd waited out storms before and been fine. He went online and looked at the storm, which at that point took up the entire Gulf of Mexico on the Weather Channel's map.

"I'd never seen anything like it," he told me. "And I said we had to go."

They loaded their dog, Rufus, one old violin, two accordions, a viola, a cello, and themselves into two old Volvos, and headed to Lafayette, where they planned to stay with friends for what they thought would be a few days.

"The three-day stay turned into an odyssey," he said.

As the storm and the flooding in New Orleans unfolded, those days turned into weeks, and then months.

"I had a lot of conflicted feelings," he said. "I had no money; I had no savings. We live month to month, like a lot of musicians. So I got some new phones and business cards, tried to make a new life."

Eventually, the family ended up buying a house in Lafayette and spending two years there. Jonno worked to get musical gigs around Lafayette, and he also began teaching occasional fiddle classes. The kids started school in Lafayette, and Maria began teaching art. In short, it looked like they had started a new life, leaving behind their old one in New Orleans. But Jonno's thoughts kept drifting back to the city. He'd returned regularly, beginning with the time when he snuck back into the city two weeks after the hurricane. At first, he didn't know if water had gotten into the house.

"Just because the water leveled off at three feet didn't mean it didn't get higher," he said.

When he could finally come back into his neighborhood, he discovered that the house had been spared. After that discovery, he kept returning to New Orleans, checking on the house,

feeding friends' cats, playing gigs. And gradually, the family began to formulate a plan to move back to New Orleans. They still
owned the house, after all, and they decided they wanted to return and rebuild what they and others had lost. They could have
sold the house on Arts Street and continued with their new lives.
But in July 2007, they moved back. They wanted to be a part of
the rebuilding process, and the kids wanted to be a part of the
city they loved, the city where they fit in, the city where they had
spent their childhood. Jonno and Maria got jobs in New Orleans, Jonno as talented arts facilitator in the Recovery School
District, and Maria as an art teacher at a local high school. They
saw it as part of their mission to rebuild their lives, as well as the
cultural and artistic life of the city.

Through teaching, creating art, and fiddling, they would
overcome the devastation.

Just as the French fiddle music had survived the long trek from
France, to Canada, and down to Cajun country, it had survived
Katrina. And in return, it was helping the city itself to survive.

Jonno pulled out his fiddle and told me to pull out mine. We
were going to have a little Cajun fiddle lesson.

"This is a song called 'Valse à Jean Billeaudeau,'" he said.
"This is a tune about a man, reportedly a serial killer. He started
killing his neighbors. He had no motive, because he had plenty
of land and money. He might have had some social problems he
was working out."

He played the tune, beginning with a few swinging notes and
progressing into a melodic waltz. He taught me the different part,
a little bit at a time, and I tried to imitate him, working on each
section. I struggled with the up and down notes, the swinging

notes. With every repetition, I got a little closer. I was getting better at playing and learning by ear. Patiently, Jonno played each section over and over. After a few minutes of struggling and getting closer, he had me play the tune straight through with him. He told me to play it again, and yet again. I did, over and over, until finally the swinging Cajun notes began to feel comfortable under my fingers.

"So put it all together and convince me that I could dance to it," he said, just like Charlene had said in the Irish fiddle workshop.

I tried again, trying to capture the tune's spirit.

"Here," he said. "I'll burn you a CD of all my music."

He played with his iTunes for a while, converting some of his recordings to MP3s, and then burned hundreds of them onto a CD.

"Take these, and listen to them," he said. "That's the only way to learn. Just keep listening."

∽

After a while, Maria came home from the Buddhist center, and Jonno introduced us. Maria had dark hair and warm, dark eyes. She smiled at me, making me feel instantly welcome and part of the family.

"You want some lunch?" she asked.

"Sure," I said.

She laid out pizza that Jonno had baked earlier, along with a salad.

"I loved your painting on the cover of the CD," I told her.

"Thanks," she said. She said that art had helped her to make sense of everything that had happened to them with Katrina and afterward, and that the floating houses represented how uprooted everyone in New Orleans had felt during and after the storm.

"Buddhist teachings of impermanence really seem to have resonance with all of this," I said. "Buddhism must have helped you to survive."

"Yeah," she said. "You know, it really has." She had a calmness about her, a sense of careful meditation around every one of her words.

We talked about the Recovery School District, where they worked, and about the recovery process in New Orleans. They were deeply involved in this recovery process; it was a central part of their lives. Jonno and Maria were a healing force in a place that desperately needed healing. Their house had so much healing energy in the air, in fact, that I, in the process of losing my husband, my prior life, and my sense of certainty about the world, felt myself absorbing it and feeling better, just being in their presence. They were helping *me* to recover. I started feeling bad, in fact, that I didn't have anything to offer to this family at all. I'd come, and spent a morning with them, and eaten their lunch, and I hadn't even thought to bring a gift. I'd come down to this city bruised and broken and unsure of myself, alone and abandoned, and somehow I'd ended up in this warm, light yellow arts-and-crafts house, drinking coffee and talking with a couple who seemed to be making their lives work against all odds. I felt at once grateful to them and truly hopeful for the first time in months, eating my pizza, looking out the front window at their prayer flags fluttering in the inexplicably bright sun.

Chapter 15

Fiddling Out
The Craigslist Chronicles

Just as all those fiddlers with their fiddles got off the boats and spread into the countryside, into the Appalachians, up and down the coast, out west, down south, bringing their fiddling with them, creating new fiddle styles as they went, I'd begun to realize that I, too, could adapt, change, and evolve. I could create new riffs. I'd learned a bit about all kinds of fiddling: Irish, Scottish, klezmer, bluegrass, western swing, Cajun. I'd traveled and traveled and traveled until I could travel no more. At once exhausted and energized, I returned home, back to my kids, my house, my job, and my village, ready to figure out what to do next.

My husband and I went to a few perfunctory, late-summer counseling sessions, but they ended up nowhere. We decided to file for a dissolution. I couldn't make him want to come back, and by then I didn't want him to. The marriage was over. We worked out a child care plan and a financial plan, we met with a lawyer in Zanesville, and we drew up documents that we filed with the court. The dissolution would be finalized a few months later in a startlingly simple, ten-minute session in the Muskingum County courthouse, not unlike the simple ceremony that had wedded us so many years before.

I began listening to my recordings, reading my notes, looking at my photos, trying to make sense of my whirlwind of travel and activity over the past couple of years. I played some of the tunes I'd learned for William, and he seemed genuinely interested in everything I'd gathered, everything I'd learned. I realized that this journey, perhaps, had not just been about my relationship with my mom, but also about my relationship with my son. Maybe he, too, could learn to improvise, evolve, and adapt. All of our lives, after all, were in flux, and the kids, too, would need to learn to survive.

Just as the people of New Orleans were rebuilding their lives in the wake of Hurricane Katrina, I decided I, too, could begin to clean up the mud and debris, salvage what I could, collect my thoughts, and move forward. Fiddling would be central to this recovery effort. My violin was still there for me, even if my husband and my previous life no longer were. It was a loyal, good friend. Everything I had learned about fiddling while journeying around the country could help me now, as I put together a new life, both for myself and for my kids.

A bit calmer than I had been over the past year, I realized I could actually put to use some of the skills and techniques I'd gathered. Maybe now, officially, I could call myself a fiddler.

In this spirit, I opened a new Gmail account, ohiofiddler@gmail.com, and I posted the fiddler's equivalent of a single's ad on Craigslist:

> I'm a fiddle player looking for an alt country/country/bluegrass/newgrass band in Columbus or southeastern Ohio to play with. I can also do lead or back-up vocals. Contact me at ohiofiddler@gmail.com.

Almost instantly, I started hearing from people. One of the first was a bluegrass duo in Columbus named Dottie and Clyde. Clyde (real name: Mike) told me to go to their MySpace page, listen to their songs, and see what I thought. "They're mostly old and shit," he said. I listened, and they weren't old or shit at all. They had a "D-major triad via iPod," which combined three songs in D major, "I'll Fly Away," "Will the Circle Be Unbroken," and "Down Time." They also had a song called "Wildwood Flower," and a few others. I listened, entranced. Dottie (real name: Jesse) sang, Clyde backed her up, and they played mandolin and banjo. I loved their sound, and I wanted to meet them, to jam with them.

One Sunday morning, I drove with the kids to Dottie and Clyde's apartment in Victorian Village, in a large building on the corner of Hubbard and Neil Avenue. Dottie had told me to come around back. William eyed the building warily.

"Maybe we should go?" he asked. "You don't know these people."

"Well, we'll know them in a few minutes," I said, sounding less confident than I felt. William was right. I *didn't* know these people. It was one thing to meet strangers in New Orleans when I was by myself, but another thing to drag the kids along with me. I almost turned back, but I thought, *We've come this far, we might as well meet them.* They'd sounded nice on the phone, after all.

The kids and I slowly and cautiously climbed the steep, creaky wooden stairs at the back of the building, trying to find their apartment. Finally, at the top, we saw them on their porch. Dottie turned out to be a tiny young woman who looked fifteen but was probably in her twenties. She was also, I'd find out, five months pregnant. She wore glasses and had a sweet face and a large, rich voice. Her husband, Clyde, who also looked young and wore glasses, was thin and kind. They brought out their guitars and banjos and mandolins, and I pulled out my fiddle, and we jammed out there on their deck, looking out over the nearby roofs of Victorian Village. Or rather, they jammed and I tried to keep up, tried to follow their chord progressions. The kids sat on folding chairs nearby, watching and listening with varying degrees of boredom and fascination over the next hour.

As we drove home, William said he liked the version of "Will the Circle Be Unbroken" that we played.

"It was cool, wasn't it?" I said, surprised that he'd been listening that closely. "It was fun to play."

"Do you have the music for it?" he asked me.

"No, I just did it by ear," I told him, looking back at him, and I could see he looked amazed. Finally, after all this time, I had his attention. I wasn't just his crazy mom, but someone who might have something interesting or useful to teach him.

"By *ear*?" he said.

"Yeah," I said. "I just listened, and then I played."

At home, William got out his violin and asked me to teach him the song. I got out mine and I just started playing it, and then improvising a bit on the melody, adding some double-stops and ornaments.

"See?" I asked, returning again to the simple melody, this time playing it slowly for him to see how it went. "It starts on a D, and then you go from there."

He noodled with it for a few minutes, and eventually we played along together. He picked out a note here, a phrase there, and after a while he could play the whole tune, and he even began to change it up a bit. Together my son and I were creating music. We were fiddling in the truest sense: not simply playing a tune out of a fiddle book, but listening, imitating, improvising. It felt good, playing with him. It felt important, as if we'd reached a moment of communication, a point at which he was learning something that would help him, too, in the future. He smiled a bit when we were done playing.

"Thanks," he said.

I touched his arm. "Sure," I said. "It was fun. We can do that some more, you know."

He nodded, and I realized that maybe we'd crossed into new territory. I'd started fiddling for my mom, but now I was fiddling as much for myself, and for my children, and for the future of my family.

∽◌

Another musician to contact me through my Craigslist listing was Hayseed, who told me he'd had a band in Nashville, had recorded a few CDs, and now was putting together a new band in Columbus. He needed a fiddle player, and he wondered if I'd like to try out.

"Are you playing anywhere around town where I could hear you?" he asked. "Or could you send me a recording of yourself?"

I first answered that I wasn't playing anywhere, and I didn't have any recordings, but then I remembered I *had* recorded "Southwest Swing" at the fiddle camp, so I e-mailed that along to him. He didn't comment on it, but he told me to take a look at his website, hayseedsings.com, and see if I'd be interested in playing with him. He also sent me MP3s of four of his songs, "Cold Feet," "Consider This," "Learn My Lesson," and "There Is a Light." I listened to them, picking out and practicing the fiddle parts. A few days later, we lined up a time for me to practice with the band on a Wednesday night in Grandview.

I realized I'd need to electrify my violin if I was going to be playing with bands. I wanted to keep playing my acoustic violin, but I needed a pickup so I could plug it into an amplifier. I called the Loft Violin Shop and they said they had a slightly used Fishman V-200 Professional Violin Pickup that they'd sell me for $100.

In the shop, the familiar wood and varnish smell hit me. The man behind the counter was a quiet man with a beard who clearly spent his days repairing violins carefully and artfully. I didn't see David or Charlene around. It looked like a quiet late afternoon at the Loft.

"What can I do for you?" he asked.

"I put a pickup for my violin on hold," I said.

He pulled out a little black box with FISHMAN written along the bottom and a purple stripe on the middle. "I think this is it," he said. "Let me see your violin."

I got it out, and he worked on it for a while, slipping the pickup in to the curving groove of the bridge, and attaching the plug, where the cable goes in, onto the side of the instrument. He went around to the front and plugged it into an amp, plucking the strings and adjusting its settings.

"I think I've got it," he said. "Want to try it out?"

I drew my bow across the strings, and a sound blazed out of the amp. I sounded, I thought, like a rock star. I liked this pickup. It felt like my violin had been made anew.

When I got home that night, I updated my Facebook status: "Vivian is electrified and amplified."

I drove slowly through the neighborhood of small, modest houses on Columbus's northwest side, looking for the address Hayseed had given me. And as I did so, I started once again having second thoughts. Here I'd found this guy on the Internet, or he'd found me, from my posting on Craigslist. Could I trust him? Like I'd done earlier in the summer in New Orleans, and with Dottie and Clyde, I'd arranged to go to a stranger's house with little to go on but a few e-mails. I parked the van and looked at the houses on the street, with their overgrown yards and cracked sidewalks. I walked up and down the street, carrying my violin and feeling conspicuous, but I couldn't find the right house. I walked a few times past a house with no number on it, and I decided eventually that it had to be the one. I steeled myself and went around back, like Hayseed had told me to do, opened the gate in the chain-link fence, and knocked on the back door, calling out, "Hello! Is anyone home?" Silence. I called out again, and then walked back into the little yard, looking at the flowers in well-kept beds. I knocked again on the door, for all the world like Clarice in *Silence of the Lambs,* and it dawned on me that I could very well be entering a trap. A man finally answered the door, and he looked harmless enough, wearing jeans and a T-shirt.

"Hi," he said. "Are you Vivian?"

I nodded.

"I'm the guitarist," he said. "Have a seat. Want something to drink?"

"Sure, thanks," I said. "A glass of water would be fine."

He went back into the house and returned with a beer for himself and a glass of water for me.

"Hayseed's not here yet," he said. "Maybe I'll check to see where he is."

He called Hayseed on his cell phone and talked for a few minutes.

"She's here; we're waiting," he said into the phone. "Uh, okay, we'll see you soon."

"He's stuck in traffic," he said. "He works at Nationwide Insurance, and he's coming here straight from work."

"Okay," I said. "Sounds fine."

We talked about his flower garden while I sipped my water and he sipped his beer. A little later, Hayseed arrived. He was a large guy with a friendly face and a beard.

"So, you must be Vivian," he said, stretching out his large hand for me to shake.

"So, you must be Hayseed," I said in return. We shook hands, and he settled himself on a seat across from me.

"How long have you been playing fiddle?" he asked, sizing me up. I'd gotten used to being sized up.

"Well, I started on classical violin when I was nine, but I've only been learning fiddle the last year or so," I said.

He nodded, studying my face.

I told him about O'Connor's camp outside of Nashville, and how I'd been learning country and bluegrass fiddling, how I appreciated the opportunity to try out for his band. He looked at me coolly, and I thought of that ram's head scroll back at Mountain Heir.

"Let's run through some songs," he said. We played through all of the songs he'd e-mailed me. He had a strong voice, and I struggled to keep up, accompanying him as background, and then stumbling into solos when he nodded in my direction. I tried to remember how the fiddling had gone on the recordings, how it had swirled in and out of the melodies. I knew in the back of my mind that it didn't matter, that I needed to improvise my own fiddling, that this wasn't just a matter of copying something

I had heard, but still I tried to remember what the fiddlers had done in those recordings.

At one point I mentioned that there hadn't been any fiddling on the recording of "Cold Feet," so I wasn't sure what to do. Hayseed looked at me, bemused, a smile faintly playing on his lips.

"Well, then I guess you're just going to have to make something up, aren't you?" he said mockingly. I could see that he wondered about me and questioned my ability to keep up with his band. And suddenly, I was wondering the same thing. Maybe I wasn't as much of a true fiddler as I thought.

A few minutes later, the rest of the band started straggling in. The long-haired, thirty-something bassist told a story about how he'd been driving his motorcycle across the country, and around the Great Lakes, before getting some beers and passing them around to the rest of the band.

"Want one?" the bass player asked me.

"No, I'll just stick with my water," I said, realizing immediately that I'd made a faux pas. Of course I needed to have a beer. But by then it was too late.

"Okay, suit yourself," he said.

"I had a lady fiddler in my band once," Hayseed said. "She worked real well with us. I don't have anything against lady fiddlers."

I heard between the lines, though: *She drinks water. She plays classical violin. She's afraid to improvise.* He didn't find this particular lady fiddler all that impressive.

After some more small talk, we migrated to the basement to begin our practice session. The dark, dank basement had a low ceiling, with little Christmas lights hung around the walls. A drum set, a collection of amps, several microphones, and a tangle of cords all crowded the small space. I worked my way over to the corner, plugging my violin into the amp. After tuning up and messing around for a few minutes, we began the set, playing the same songs that Hayseed and the guitarist and I had played out on the porch. The band seemed to know these songs well. There in the dark, low-ceilinged basement, I did my best to keep up with all of the instruments, riding on the wild roller coaster of sound. Sometimes I struggled and floundered, faking it. Other times, though, I hit a jamming groove that went beyond copying what I remembered from the recordings and into new territory. Sometimes I'd look over at the bass player, and we'd hit a groove together and he'd smile. I felt all right.

Around 10:30, things began to wind down, and I told Hayseed I had to go.

"Sure, we're wrapping up anyway," he said. I unplugged my violin and put it away in its case.

As I was leaving, I said, "So will you call me to let me know about your next band practice?"

"Well, yeah, we'll see," Hayseed said in a "don't call us we'll call you" sort of tone. "I have another fiddle player to try out, a cousin of one of the band members. We'll try him out at a gig next week, and then I'll get back with you and let you know what I think."

"Sounds good," I said.

"I really like your, what do you call it, your *tone*," Hayseed said in a way that made me think that maybe he really didn't. Or perhaps I sounded too much like a violinist, and not enough like a fiddler. *Tone* wasn't something fiddlers typically worried a whole hell of a lot about. "You sound real good."

"Thanks," I said. "I had a great time."

"I'll be in touch," Hayseed said as I climbed the stairs.

"Sounds good," I said, making my way back out through the porch, the flower garden, and to the car.

I drove home happy that night, though I knew that I probably wouldn't be asked to return to Hayseed's band. The fiddling that I'd been dabbling in had begun to seem real, something that I could do, even if I wasn't yet good enough for this band. I felt like I'd taken up residence in a foreign country and had been picking up the language, without even realizing it. Now it surprised me to be putting together a few sentences. I might be a lady fiddler who drinks water, but that was better than nothing.

A few weeks later, I got a message through Facebook from Hayseed, telling me he was sorry, but he'd decided to go with another fiddler for the band, the cousin of a band member who had lots of bluegrass experience. He said he was happy to have met me and that he looked forward to hearing me around town.

For a few days, I was crushed. What had I done? What could I have done differently? But then I picked myself up, dusted myself off, and went forward. If fiddling had taught me anything, it was not to give up.

Chapter 16

Jamming

Remembering what Leigh Ann had told me at the Highland Games about the folk jams she held at McDonald's in her West Virginia town, that summer I arranged a folk jam through the New Concord Area Arts & Recreation District, a local organization with which I'd been involved. It would be held at the Jitterbug Coffee House, a little casual coffeeshop on a side alley off Main Street in the village's downtown, a small wood-frame building that had become the soul of the village since it had opened a few years before. With wood floors, antiques, and paintings on the wall from local artists, it had become a place where faculty, students, and people from the town could come, mingle, and just hang out. I'd sent press releases to *The Daily Jeffersonian* in Cambridge, and to the *Times Recorder* in Zanesville. I didn't know what would happen, but I hoped to coax some people out of the woodwork. This was a moment when I could use fiddling to finally connect to my rural Appalachian village and its culture. I hadn't met any other musicians locally, but I knew they must be there, somewhere. It was just a matter of casting a line out and seeing who I could reel in. I had no idea what to expect, but I hoped at least a few people would show up.

Sure enough, people came. Tom, a quiet older gentleman, played banjo. He sat on one of the chairs on the side of the room and didn't say much, but he kept playing. Charlie, who was probably in his seventies or eighties—with a pleasant face and a handsome smile—wore a red button-down shirt and a black baseball cap. He played guitar and brought with him a wealth of old songs that he could pull out and play. Perry, who told us he played contemporary and old-time gospel in his church, played banjo, mandolin, and guitar. For years I didn't feel like I fit in with the people around here, but now that I was with some of them, I got along just fine. I wasn't an outsider. I was one of them, hanging out, playing a little music on a Saturday morning.

We sat around in the black cushioned chairs arranged in a rough circle in the main room of the coffee house, playing, jamming, and improvising for two hours. I drank a mocha frappe with an extra shot of espresso, which kept me nicely caffeinated. Each time one of them called out a tune, I turned around to my laptop to record it in GarageBand, wanting to keep MP3s of everything we played so I could practice them at home. They all waited patiently while, like an awkward ethnographer, I set up the software to record each song.

Charlie played all sorts of songs, including strange ones like "Flying Saucer Man," which told a story about a trucker seeing aliens, and "Lover's Dream," which he said he'd written back in 1941. Tom played a few banjo solos, and Perry played several gospel tunes. As we played, I listened and tried to improvise along with them, surprised at how naturally the notes came. There at that folk jam that morning, I felt like I'd turned a corner. I was doing it. I was improvising. Sometimes I'd make a mistake, but I'd quickly get out of it and back on a note that fit the chord. I found there was no way to truly make a mistake, in fact. Even notes that weren't quite right could be made to fit with a song. I tried various things, playing melody along with Charlie as he sang, and accompanying him with short chops that I'd learned at the fiddle camp. When I listened to the recordings later, I realized that the short chops worked better with the fiddle coming in as a solo in between verses, a technique I'd make sure to try at the next jam session.

In the other room, some friends of mine from the college, Amy and Alistair, Dave and Sandy, and Bil, sat and listened to the music. At the end of each song, they'd clap, and sometimes Amy raised her thumb in approval.

We ended the jam with "Wiggle Wiggle," a song from Charlie. I tried, largely unsuccessfully, to imitate the melody on my violin. Charlie humored me, though, smiling and laughing as I struggled with the song's bluesy, bendy notes.

As we wrapped up, I got Charlie's and Tom's and Perry's phone numbers, so next time I organized one of these jams I could call them and let them know. Charlie pulled out a CD of his playing and signed it to me, "To Vivian Wagner, From Charlie Weaver," with a ball point pen on the inside of the CD's cover.

As we left, Charlie said, "You're a great fiddler; you're perfect, just perfect."

"Really?" I said. "Thanks, Charlie, that's so nice."

"Well, I know a real fiddler when I hear one," he said, getting in his car. "See you at the next one!"

I waved as he drove away, feeling elated. *A real fiddler.* I had finally arrived. Or, at least, I'd arrived in New Concord, where I'd been all along. For the first time, I was starting to feel at home here in this little village in rural Appalachia. Starting to feel like I spoke the language, or at least one of the languages. Starting to feel like I belonged.

Chapter 17

Miles to Go

One morning that fall, as I hurriedly made copies before class, I saw Laura, a history professor at the college who had a certainty about the world that I envied and respected. She had no-nonsense gray eyes and straight shoulder-length hair, and she wore sensible yet fashionable shoes. She'd always been on the fringes of my circle of friends, but I'd never gotten to know her well. I smiled and said, "Hi, good morning," before turning back to the copy machine.

"Hey, Vivian," she said. "Want to come play with us?"

I turned around and looked at her blankly. *Play with us?* At first I thought she meant a playgroup with the kids, since she had a young daughter, Kate. It had been years since I took my kids to playgroups, and though I vaguely remembered the existence of such things, I was now in another world, taking the kids to martial arts, violin lessons, piano lessons, soccer. And I had a few new beats lately: negotiating with their dad for kid drop-offs and pick-ups, working out child care schedules, dividing up time. It seemed like another lifetime when I took toddlers to playgroups.

Then the thought dawned on me: *She's talking about her band.* I had heard about the band, last called something like Lament for Pluto, which had also included a philosophy professor who had since moved away, as well as Jim, a biology professor, and Laura's husband, Greg, a history professor at the University of Akron. I knew they played indie rock, but I had never thought of them as needing a fiddle player. I'd always thought of fiddle as belonging to country or bluegrass bands, even though everything I'd learned in my travels suggested there were no real limits to fiddle playing, that it could fit in just about any genre. I guess, mainly, it had never occurred to me that they'd want to play with *me*. They were cool, and I wasn't.

At least, not *cool enough.*

"Sure, I'd love to," I said, flattered, impressed, not sure how to respond.

"Great," she said. "How about next Saturday? I'll get you copies of the music we've been playing, and Jim can make you a CD. Do you sing, too?"

"Yeah, I like to sing," I said. "Mostly, I've sung folk songs by myself with my guitar, and in choirs. But I've never sung in a band."

"Good, then you can sing lead instead of me," she said.

"Okay," I said. "That sounds fun."

A few days later, Jim put a CD of the songs they'd been working in my box, and Laura gave me printouts of the words and chords. The CD had thirteen songs, comprising Bruce Springsteen, Tom Petty and the Heartbreakers, and the Rolling Stones. And a few from indie rock bands with a soft, edgy sound that I didn't know anything about, like the Skydiggers and PJ Harvey. At home, I listened to the songs, fiddling along in the background. I wasn't sure how I'd fit in to all of this, but I was excited about trying.

The next Saturday evening, I lined up a babysitter to stay with the kids. Jim came to my house in his dark blue truck, and I climbed in, stacking my violin on top of his electric guitar behind the seats. Jim had been a friend for many years, but we'd never been particularly close. I'd seen him at parties and around, but I'd never sat and talked with him very much. For the past few years, I hadn't even been to many parties, preferring instead to stay home with the kids while my husband went out. Jim had turned fifty the year before, and he had golden brown hair that always hung around his head in a kind of calculated messiness. He directed the college's conservation science program and coordinated the college's scholarly relationship with the Wilds, an animal research organization south of New Concord in Cumberland. He wore jeans and a worn leather jacket, and his thin, lined face had a rakish boyishness.

"It's great to have you along," he said in his casual, folksy way, a hint of a genteel Virginia accent in his voice. "If you don't mind, I have to stop to get some beer at the Cooler." We stopped at this liquor store just on the eastern edge of New Concord. The village is dry, so the Cooler and a drive-through joint called Save-a-Step just outside the village limits are the only places to buy alcohol nearby. A sign by the road in front of the Cooler read LIVE BAIT. We pulled in on the dirt road up to the little brick building surrounded by pieces of machinery, earth-moving equipment, and an assortment of trucks and cars. Jim went inside to buy the beer while I waited in the pickup. Back in the truck we resumed our journey to Cambridge, where Laura and Greg live.

"I'm looking forward to playing with you guys," I said awkwardly. "I'm not sure exactly what I'm doing. I've only ever played with a band one time, and they didn't ask me to come back."

"That's fine," he said, laughing. "You can play whatever you like. We're pretty casual. We really don't want to stress out about performances right now. We're just looking to have a good time."

Laura and Greg lived in a large, two-story house in an older section of Cambridge, next door to an empty lot they also owned. Their house had a side door with stairs leading up to the studio. Jim pulled up out front, and Greg came out and helped us unload our instruments and guide us upstairs.

"Welcome to the band!" Greg said.

"Thanks," I replied.

Greg was smart and funny, with light brown hair and a friendly face. Like Jim, he'd been on the fringe of my circle of friends, but I'd never really gotten to know him. Lugging the various instruments and amps, we climbed the stairs to their studio, a small room at the front of their house on the second floor, with windows looking out over the street.

"Hey," Laura said when we came in. "Kate's just down for bed. Let's play! Do you want a glass of wine?"

I said a glass of water would be fine, and she fetched it along with the wine for herself. The guys opened their beers. Greg settled at his drum set; Jim tuned his guitar; and I got out my violin and plugged it into their amp, trying to act like I knew what I was doing.

That first night we ran through Tom Petty's "Runnin' Down a Dream"; the Skydiggers' "Darkness and Doubt" and "Joanne"; the Rolling Stones' "Wild Horses"; and PJ Harvey's "You Said Something." In some of the songs I fiddled, trying to play a mixture of backup and solos. In others, like "Wild Horses," I sang along with Jim, attempting to match my voice to his. It was wonderful, freeing, and fun. Lucky for me and my scrambling attempts to play, the band didn't emphasize perfection as much as having a good time, and I found myself able to blend and move with them in ways I hadn't predicted I'd be able to do. It turned out that my and Jim's voices went well together, the roughness of his voice and the smoothness of mine complementing each other.

We're onto something, I thought. *I'm supposed to be here.*

Usually I don't think in terms of fate. I don't think things happen for a reason. But that night at Laura's house, I started getting an inkling of what people mean when they talk about fate. Everything about it felt right.

Fiddling, though, had also taught me to improvise. With improvising, you don't know what's going to happen, and you do your best with what's thrown at you. You might know the chords, the general progression, and the melody, but you don't know exactly what's going to happen at any moment. You simply take what comes your way and make the best of it. So whether or not playing in the band was meant to be, it *was* something I could incorporate into my life, something I could riff on. I was learning how to not rely on printed music or predictable scripts. I was still a long way from knowing exactly what I was doing as a fiddler, and I still felt like I was making everything up as I went along. I'd been learning to improvise gradually, dabbling in many different styles—Irish, Scottish, bluegrass, western swing, klezmer, and Cajun—but I was starting to be able to make something new from these influences. They were, as Mark O'Connor would say, cross-pollinating.

So I had landed, happily, unexpectedly, somewhere between fate and improvisation.

We wrapped up the session around 10 p.m. and put our instruments away.

"That was great," Greg said.

"Yeah, I really enjoyed it," I said. "I love singing with you, Jim."

Jim smiled. "Me, too, with you," he said. "I think this is going to work. And it's great having the fiddle in there. That adds a whole new dimension to the band."

We talked about our rehearsal schedule, finally settling on a Saturday evening in two weeks. We said our good-byes and loaded our instruments into Jim's truck and headed back to New Concord.

"So, I think that went pretty well," Jim said on the drive home.

"I do, too," I agreed, feeling a bit less awkward. "Thanks so much for inviting me."

"I think you're a natural fit for the band," he said. "I think it's going to work well."

The band practiced regularly through the fall, every Friday or Saturday night or so. We'd choose a few new songs here and there, and my bandmates would ask, "Why don't you throw a little fiddle in there?" I'd listen to the chords, or to the recordings we had, and I'd try to improvise. What I played didn't always work, but I didn't mind. Over the next months, the band's repertoire grew, and I introduced a few tunes: Gillian Welch's "Whiskey Girl," a good song because she sings in my range and because I could easily add in fiddle solos; and Lucinda Williams's "Pineola," an alt-country song about a teenage suicide. We began to feel more and more comfortable with each other, and increasingly, I realized I had found a musical home. I had found a group I could stay with, grow with, play with into the future. We weren't sure, still, about when, if ever, we would perform. It was, at the time, just good to be getting together, playing, making music, and learning about each other.

Our band was nameless for a while, but eventually we decided to call ourselves Whiskey Beach, after a beach in Delaware that Jim liked. None of the rest of us had ever been there, but Whiskey Beach seemed to capture something of our hybrid, alt-country spirit.

A few months after I started playing with the band, Laura and I met for lunch on campus.

"Do you think it's going okay with me in the band?" I asked. "I mean, I know you guys were together for a while without me, and I'm enjoying it, but I want to make sure that you think I fit in."

"It's like you've always been in the band," she said with that certainty in her voice that I'd always admired. When Laura said something, it was as good as true.

Moore's Music Emporium in Bridgeport, Ohio, on the far eastern edge of the state near Wheeling, West Virginia, is a small shop on a narrow road near the river. Just off the interstate, past Appalachian houses with knickknacks and sofas on the porches nestled into the rough, sharp hillsides, Moore's is a small-town, independently owned music store in a nineteenth-century brick building.

On the Saturday after Thanksgiving, Greg, Jim, and I took my minivan on a road trip to Moore's to look for band equipment.

We'd just gotten paid, and it was a brilliant, sunny fall day. A good day for a road trip. Most of the leaves had fallen from the trees, and the hills spread before us, brown and gold. I put on my sunglasses, and we set off east of Cambridge on Interstate 70 in the early afternoon. The kids were at Cleveland with their grandparents for the Thanksgiving holiday, so I was free that day, and I felt happy to be with these two guys, my friends and bandmates.

Inside, Moore's had a homely feel. It was packed with guitars, drum sets, mandolins, banjos. We went into a back room and found a monitor we liked, on sale for $129. I found a black guitar strap, a pick-up for my guitar, two picks, and a Blues Harp E harmonica. Jim picked out a portable amp with a brown leather cover that made it look like a piece of vintage luggage. It had two pickups, which we would be able to use when practicing together. It cost $319, but he assured us it would be worth it; he could use it on his own, or we could use it together, or we might even be able to use it with the band.

Before we left, Greg looked at a dulcimer. It was $99, and the label inside said it had been made in Romania.

"I really want to try new instruments," he said. "On the one hand I want a new guitar, but I also want to try new sounds. And I love this dulcimer."

It had dark stained wood on the sides and a light wooden top, carved with heart-like shapes, and it came with a carrying case. We tried it out, strumming the drone strings and the melody strings. The guy working in the store picked out "Simple Things" on it for us, showing us how to hold it in our laps.

"You know, we might want to try to find a locally made dulcimer," I said. "Seeing as how we're in Appalachia; there's got to be somewhere to find those."

"Yeah, you're right," Greg said. "I just really like it."

While he looked at it, I got a mandolin down from the wall and started strumming it. Mandolins have the same strings as violins, but they're held like a guitar. I tried to get a few chords out of it that sounded right. I knew what Greg meant; it would be great to bring in some other sounds into the band. We could learn other instruments, try new things. Greg smiled as he played the dulcimer, and I felt a heady sense of possibility and promise in the air. We'd, all of us, make it. We were onto something. The world, suddenly, seemed limitless, open, and free. More than I ever thought it would be.

We paid for our purchases, loaded everything into the van, and started back home, through the Appalachian hills, past forests of maple and oak, past hollows and fields, the late afternoon light streaming in through the windshield.

I wanted to work on some original material for Whiskey Beach to play, so I asked my friend Jane if she had any poems I could set to music. She said she'd rather get together over red wine and write a song, so we set aside a night to do that.

One cold January night, in the middle of a two-week-long arctic front that had slashed down through the country from Canada, she brought her daughter Iris over, along with lentil soup she had made in a slow cooker. We ate the soup, accompanied by slices of tomato with Swiss cheese and a loaf of my homemade French bread. After we ate, we sat in the living room by the fire, feeling its warmth and listening to the crackle of the logs.

"I don't have any idea how to write a song," I told Jane as we sat by the sputtering fire. Miles lay stretched on the couch, staring at us, waiting to see what we'd do. I'd never written a song, and I didn't even know how to begin.

"Well, I don't, either," she said. "So we're in the same boat."

I pulled out my guitar and violin. Rose and Iris escaped into Rose's room to play with their Webkinz on the computer. William sat on the couch by me, watching and listening. I strummed a few chords on my guitar: A, D, a modified version of E.

"That sounds good," said Jane. "Play those again."

I did, creating a base, a progression, something to build on.

"That sounds to me like the moon," Jane said. "I've been thinking about the moon lately."

"Hmmm," I said. "Okay."

"You know, the moon is made mostly of lava," she said.

We drank our wine, pondering that for a minute, watching the fire. We pulled out an atlas of the universe that I'd gotten William for Christmas. Maps of the moon's surface showed all the *lunar maria*, which were once thought to have been formed by water, hence the use of the Latin word, "mare," meaning lake. In fact, though, the lakes of the moon were formed by ancient floods of lava.

"Why don't you come up with a tune first, and then I'll come up with some words," Jane said.

So I played around with a tune, picking up my fiddle for a few minutes and then switching back to guitar. Gradually, I settled on a tune; Jane began to write words about the moon, space, distance. Iris and Rose popped in now and then and contributed words and ideas.

"What would the stars do to the sky?" Jane wondered out loud.

"Um, they'd polish it?" Iris asked, without thinking.

"Yeah," Jane said. "*Polish*. That's good!"

Iris smiled, and then she and Rose ran back to Rose's room.

After a while of jotting down words, fiddling with melodies, and rearranging, we came up with a song called "Miles," named partly after my dog and partly after the vast distances in space.

Jane wrote out the lyrics on a piece of notebook paper:

> *Moon, I thought you were following me,*
> *But then you were gone,*
> *Then you were gone.*

> *Stars, I thought you'd be here tonight,*
> *You polished the air,*
> *You polished the air.*

> *Sky surprises us.*
> *Signs don't rise up.*
> *Here all alone,*
> *Where light years are known.*

> *Love, you said that you knew me.*
> *You promised a sun,*
> *You promised a sun.*

> *Love, I thought you were following me,*
> *But then you were gone,*
> *Then you were gone.*

We practiced the new song a few times. I played guitar a bit, and then I picked up my violin and fiddled in between the verses.

"Could I play, too?" William asked.

"Sure," I said, and he got his violin. I played through the basic melody for him, and then he imitated it. His ear had been developing since that day we'd played "Will the Circle Be Unbroken" together. He and I were both getting more comfortable picking up melodies by ear.

"You can improvise off of that basic tune," I said, playing a few riffs for him. He noodled around, giving it a try, smiling, getting in the groove. I'd been happy to see that he'd really been getting into playing his violin lately. He gained more technical proficiency and had arrived at a point where playing violin was not just work; it was also fun. He seemed especially interested in trying out this improvising that Mom kept talking about, too.

After a while, Rose and Iris came back to the living room, and they listened to us practicing the song.

"Why are all songs about love?" Rose asked after one of our run-throughs.

"A lot of them are, aren't they?" I said, feeling I needed to say more to her, but not knowing what to say, or how to say it. "I guess it's just one of those things people feel they need to sing about."

We decided to do a final performance of the song and record it on GarageBand, so we'd remember how it went, and also so I could send an MP3 to the band. Rose, Iris, and Jane listened while William and I performed.

As we played, there was a hint of bluegrass, a hint of Irish, and a hint of Cajun lilt in the notes, but the music wasn't firmly in any one of these genres. The past several years of traveling around the country, meeting fiddlers and immersing myself in various fiddle cultures began to find expression in that moment. The journey, after all, had only partly been about learning to fiddle. It had also been about being grounded in the past, being humble, learning from those around me, and developing grit, tenacity, and fearlessness. Skills, perhaps, that my mom had wanted me to learn all along, in order to better deal with the unexpected, unpredictable turns that my life would inevitably take. I still had a long way to go until I'd be anything like an expert fiddler, but I was getting somewhere. Like fiddling itself, I was evolving. And like fiddling, I would survive. My kids would survive. We would make it.

And so, for a few minutes, William and I scattered notes around the living room, playing around with the melody, making it up as we went along, spinning sound out of nothing, into something new.

Acknowledgments

Thanks to all my violin and fiddle teachers, past and present, who taught me how to play, and so much more. Thanks to everyone I met along this journey who befriended me, took me into their homes, fed me, and gave me insights into the world of fiddling. Thanks to my unsurpassed agent, Laurie Abkemeier, for her wisdom, friendship, and persistence, and to my editors at Kensington Books, Danielle Chiotti, Mike Shohl, and Amy Pyle, and production editor Arthur Maisel for their good eyes and sharp wits. Thanks to my close readers and friends, David Arnold, Suzanne Farrell Smith, Timothy Rogers, and Amy Rushton, for helping me to see my story with fresh eyes. Thanks to Marcia Weiss and Kathy Wesley for their multifaceted guidance. Thanks to Greg Miller of Uncabaret Laboratories for helping me understand how to tell a story. Thanks to my writing mentors and teachers, Rebecca McClanahan, Michael Czyzniejewski, David Lazar, Lee K. Abbott, Carol Bly, Anya Achtenberg, Laurie Wagner, Gretchen Clark, Amanda Castleman, Sheila Bender,

Gloria Kempton, Jay Cooke, Rita Rosenberg, Speer Morgan and Lynda Zwinger, for teaching me about this craft.

Thanks to Muskingum University for a faculty development grant that helped make this project possible, and thanks to Donna Edsall and all of the members of Muskingum University's English Department for their consistent, unwavering support. Thanks to Jane Varley, Gary Atkins, Alistair Hattingh, Bil and Katie Kerrigan, Jim Dooley, Laura Hilton, Greg Wilson, Robin Densmore, Danny Ingold, Will and Sommer Mullins, Tim and Rachel Pollock, Jeff Harman, Diane Rao, David Tabachnick, Sandy Rucker-Tabachnick, Jon Hale, Laura Schumann, Harsha Abeyaratne, Richard Williamson, Leigh Range, Sheila Ellenberger, Andrew Whitis, Siobhan Senier, Jill Bergman, Lisa Stowe, Alison Weir, Amy Penne, Michael Thurston, Barry Faulk, Angela Hamilton, Claire Chantell, Marcella Missirian, Beth Ina, Tim Coyne, Bruce Anderson, David Goodwillie, Suzanne Finnamore, and Lee Martin for their friendship and help of many kinds. Thanks to Facebook for connecting and reconnecting me with some of these friends. Thanks to the Jitterbug, Uppity's Coffee House, and the New Concord Public Library for giving me space to work. Thanks to Ann for her sisterhood, and for her lovely cello playing. Thanks to my mom and dad for my violin, and for my lessons, and for everything, tangible and intangible, that they have given me. And finally, thanks to my children, William and Rose, for their patience, intelligence, good humor, and unconditional love. I've learned more from them than they will ever know.

Bibliography

Farga, Franz. *Violins and Violinists*. Trans. Egon Larsen. New York: Macmillan, 1950.

Gough, Colin. "Science and the Stradivarius." PhysicsWorld.com. April 1, 2000. physicsworld.com/cws/article/print/696.

Green, Harvey. *Wood: Craft, Culture, History*. New York: Penguin, 2007.

Haigh, Chris. "Fiddling Around the World." www.fiddling around.co.uk.

———. *The Fiddle Handbook*. San Francisco: Backbeat Books, 2009.

Kolneder, Walter. *The Amadeus Book of the Violin: Construction, History, and Music*. Portland, OR: Amadeus Press, 1993.

Marchese, John. *The Violin Maker: Finding a Centuries-Old Tradition in a Brooklyn Workshop*. New York: HarperCollins, 2007.

Sapoznik, Henry. *Klezmer! Jewish Music from Old World to Our World*. New York: Schirmer Books, 1999.

Schlesinger, Kathleen. *The Precursors of the Violin Family: Records, Researches and Studies*. London: W. Reeves, 1914.

Strom, Yale. *The Book of Klezmer: The History, the Music, the Folklore*. Chicago: Chicago Review Press, 2002.

VanClay, Mary. "From Horse to Bow." *Strings*, Jan./Feb. 1995: 40–42.

Wolfe, Charles. *The Devil's Box: Masters of Southern Fiddling*. Nashville: Vanderbilt University Press, 1997.